Recommendations for Linkword

'I am happy to say that I was delighted, and very impressed with your course'
Paul Daniels

'We have found the Linkword programmes to be both effective and entertaining'
Brian Ablett, Training Development Office, British Caledonian

'The most entertaining language tutor of all: it works and it's fun'
Jack Schofield, The Guardian

'Feel free to quote me as a satisfied customer'
Michael Woodhall, Director Language Learning Centre, Manchester Business School

'It took 12 hours to teach a regime that normally takes 40 hours'
Peter Marsh, Thomson Holidays

'I was quite frankly astounded at how effective this visual imagery was as an aid to memory retention'
Lolita Taylor, Popular Computer World

'I tried the system out in German and French and was amazed at how quickly it worked'
Jan McCann, Toronto Sun

COURSE DESIGNER AND WRITER

Dr Michael M. Gruneberg, designer and writer of the Gruneberg Linkword Language Courses, is Senior Lecturer in Psychology at University College, Swansea, Wales. He has published a number of well-known books on memory, and is an organiser of two major international conferences on Practical Aspects of Memory. He has also published a number of research papers concerned with practical and theoretical aspects of memory. For the past few years he has worked with a number of linguists in designing the Gruneberg Linkword Language System.

LANGUAGE CONSULTANT

Gabriel C. Jacobs B.A., Ph.D., Lecturer in Romance Studies, University College of Swansea, Wales. Dr Jacobs has been involved for some time in the practical application of language.

Also available from Corgi Books:

LINKWORD LANGUAGE SYSTEM - ITALIAN
LINKWORD LANGUAGE SYSTEM - SPANISH
LINKWORD LANGUAGE SYSTEM - GERMAN

French

Michael M. Gruneberg

Language Consultant
Gabriel C. Jacobs

CORGI BOOKS

To John Beloff

LINKWOOD LANGUAGE SYSTEM –
FRENCH
A CORGI BOOK   0 552 13053 2

First publication in Great Britain.

PRINTING HISTORY

Corgi edition published 1987
Corgi edition reprinted 1988 (twice)

Copyright © Dr Michael Gruneberg 1987

This book is set in 9/10pt Century
by Colset Private Limited, Singapore.

Corgi Books are published by Transworld Publishers
Ltd., 61-63 Uxbridge Road, Ealing, London W5 5SA,
in Australia by Transworld Publishers (Australia)
Pty. Ltd., 15-23 Helles Avenue, Moorebank, NSW
2170, and in New Zealand by Transworld Publishers
(N.Z.) Ltd., Cnr. Moselle and Waipareira Avenues,
Henderson, Auckland.

Printed and bound in Great Britain by
The Guernsey Press Co. Ltd., Guernsey, Channel Islands.

Contents

A Foreword by Paul Daniels

As you may know I, Paul Daniels, am a professional magician, and as such am involved in the business of deception. I am also writing this foreword without ever having seen the full text of this book.

Add these two facts together and you may well wonder why or how I can speak with any degree of authority or expect to be believed when I extol the virtues of the Linkword system.

Well, the simple truth is that one Monday morning at nine a.m. I did not speak a single word of Spanish and by five p.m. on the following Friday I knew hundreds of words of Spanish! I know that is true because I counted them!! Please note the use of the word 'knew' in the last sentence . . . it was chosen deliberately . . . I knew the words positively enough to KNOW that when I said them they were the correct words. My brain reeled with the excitement of learning so much so fast. At forty-eight years of age I had finally got to the stage of being able to communicate with people of another language . . . and how they loved me for trying.

A few weeks later, with no more lessons other than my own reading of Spanish newspapers and books I went on stage and performed my act entirely in Spanish, and now I am 'all fired up' and anxious to learn more. It's wonderful.

Memory systems go back a long way, and I have read many that have suggested their methods could be applied to language learning, but this system is the first I have come across where someone has actually provided a complete system that is 'ready to go'. When you first read memory systems that use idiotic association as a memory aid it is very easy to think that the idea itself is stupid, BUT IT WORKS!!!

So, do yourself a favour and don't knock it till you have tried it. Once you have found out for yourself how to use your own imagination fully to really 'see' the mental images I am sure that like me you will be wondering why this 'game' of learning language is not taught in all our schools.

Paul Daniels

Linkword Language System – French

TEST YOURSELF WITH LINKWORD

Picture each of these images in your mind's eye for about 10 seconds

○ The French for TABLECLOTH is NAPPE
Imagine having a *NAP* on a *TABLECLOTH*.

○ The German for GENTLEMEN is HERREN
Imagine a *HERRING* dangling from the door of a *GENTLE-MEN'S* toilet.

○ The Italian for FLY is MOSCA.
Imagine *FLIES* invading *MOSCOW*.

○ The Spanish for SUITCASE is MALETA
Imagine *MY LETTER* in your *SUITCASE*.

○ The French for HEDGEHOG is HERISSON.
Imagine your *HAIRY SON* looks like a *HEDGEHOG*.

○ The German for LETTER is BRIEF.
Imagine a *BRIEF LETTER*.

○ The Italian for DRAWER is CASSETTO.
Imagine you keep *CASSETTES* in a *DRAWER*.

○ The Spanish for WAITRESS is CAMARERA.
Imagine a *WAITRESS* with a *CAMERA* slung around her neck!

NOW TURN OVER

○ What is the English for CAMARERA?   _____

○ What is the English for CASSETTO?   _____

○ What is the English for BRIEF?   _____

○ What is the English for HERISSON?   _____

○ What is the English for MALETA?   _____

○ What is the English for MOSCA?   _____

○ What is the English for HERREN?   _____

○ What is the English for NAPPE?   _____

TURN BACK FOR THE ANSWERS

Do not expect to get them all correct at the first attempt. However, if you feel you got more right than you normally would have — then this course will suit you!

INTRODUCTION

Who is Linkword for?

The short answer is that Linkword is for anyone and everyone who wants to learn the basics of a language in a hurry. Linkword is for the holidaymaker, for the business person, for school work or for pleasure. It can be used by children or by adults. Even young children who cannot read can be taught French words by a parent reading out the images.

How to Use Linkword

1] LEARNING THE WHOLE COURSE (WORDS AND GRAMMAR)

The Linkword Courses have been carefully designed to teach you a basic grammar and words in a simple step by step way that anyone can follow. After about 10—12 hours or even less, you will have a vocabulary of 350—400 words and the ability to string these words together to form sentences. The course is ideal, therefore, for the holidaymaker or business person who just wants the basics in a hurry so he or she can be understood, e.g. in the hotel, arriving at their destination, sightseeing, shopping, eating out, in emergencies, telling the time and so on.

2] LEARNING THE WORDS ONLY

If you are revising for exams and just want to boost your vocabulary, or if you are going abroad and just want to learn some words so that you can cope with emergencies say, or order a meal in a restaurant etc., then just look up the Table of Contents on page v and turn to the section you want. You can read only the pages with the words and images. You should, however test yourself to make sure that the words are "sticking".

Obviously if you only learn the words you will not be able to communicate as well as if you learn both words and grammar. However you *can* often communicate using just one word, e.g. "bill!" will communicate to the waiter that you want the bill!

One word of warning however. The words will not stick as well in your memory if they are learned as single words compared to being learned with grammar as part of the whole course.

Instructions

1] You will be presented with words like this:
The French for TABLECLOTH is NAPPE
Imagine having a NAP on a TABLECLOTH
What you do is to imagine this picture in your mind's eye as vividly as possible.

2] After you have read the image you should think about it in your mind's eye for about 10 seconds before moving on to the next word. If you do not spend enough time thinking about the image it will not stick in your memory as well as it should.

3] Sometimes the word in French and in English is the same or very similar. For example, the French for "taxi" is "taxi". When this happens you will be asked to associate the word in some way with the Eiffel Tower.

Imagine a taxi driving under the Eiffel Tower. Whenever the Eiffel Tower comes to mind, therefore, you will know the word is the same or similar in both English and French.

4] It is very important to realise that some groups of words are more difficult to learn than others. If you find this do not worry, just go on to the next set of words and forget you have had any difficulty. The important thing to appreciate is how much you *do* learn very quickly.

5] The examples given in the course may well strike you as silly and bizarre. They have deliberately been given in this way to show up points of grammar and to get away from the idea that you should remember useful phrases "parrot fashion".

6] ACCENTS

As accents can often be omitted on capital letters in French, there are no accents in this course. This has been done to help you learn quickly. However the correct accents are given in the glossary at the end of the book.

7] PRONUNCIATION

The approximate pronunciation of words is given in brackets after the word is presented for the first time.

For example: The French for CABBAGE is CHOU (SHOO)
(SHOO) is the way the word is pronounced.

When the following letters appear, in the words in brackets (pronunciation words) they sound like this.

"J" sounds like the "S" in pleasure.
"oo" sounds like a sort of "OO" sound.
"n" sounds like the "N" in fiancé.
"e" sounds like the "U" in curl.

For example

The French for garage is garage (GARAJ).
The French for skirt is jupe (JooP).
The French for rabbit is lapin (LAPAHn).
The French for the is le (Le).

Do not worry too much about these pronunciations to begin with. The approximate pronunciation given in brackets will allow you to be understood. If you would like to listen to the exact pronunciation, an audio-tape containing all the words on the course is available from Corgi Books.

Important Note

The first section of the course can basically be regarded as a training section designed to get you into the Linkword method quickly and easily. After about 45 minutes you will have a vocabulary of about 30 words and you will be able to translate sentences. Once you have finished Section I you will have the confidence to go through the rest of the course just as quickly. Animal words are used in the first section as they are a large group of "easy to image" words. Many animal words of course are useful to have as they are often met abroad, e.g. dog, cat, etc., or they are edible!

Finally . . .

When it comes to translating sentences the answers are given at the foot of the page. You may find it useful to cover up the answers before you tackle the translations.

Section 1 ANIMALS

N.B. The word on the right-hand side of the page (IN BRACKETS) is the way the word is pronounced.

THINK OF EACH IMAGE IN YOUR MIND'S EYE FOR ABOUT TEN SECONDS

○ The French for RABBIT is LAPIN   (LAPAHn)*
   Imagine a rabbit LAPPING at a bowl of water.

○ The French for CAT is CHAT   (SHA)
   Imagine the late SHAH of Iran, with a black
   cat on his knee.

○ The French for GOAT is CHEVRE   (SHEVR)
   Imagine driving your CHEVI to the Levee
   with a goat in the back.

○ The French for HORSE is CHEVAL   (SHeVAL)
   Imagine a diSHEVELLED looking horse.

○ The French for ANIMAL is ANIMAL   (ANEEMAL)
   Imagine ANIMALS looking out from the
   Eiffel Tower.

○ The French for HEDGEHOG is HERISSON   (AYREESO-n)
   Imagine your HAIRY SON looking like a
   hedgehog.

○ The French for COW is VACHE   (VASH)
   Imagine trying to WASH a cow.

○ The French for DOG is CHIEN   (SHEE AHn)
   Imagine a dog with a SHEEN on its coat.

○ The French for DEER is CERF   (SER)
   Imagine a SERF bringing a dead deer to his
   master.

○ The French for GOOSE is OIE   (WA)
   Imagine a goose hanging from a WIRE in a
   butcher's shop.

*Remember that a small 'n' in the pronunciation always sounds like the 'n' in fiance.

YOU CAN WRITE YOUR ANSWERS IN

○ What is the English for OIE? (WA) — _GOOSE_

○ What is the English for CERF? (SER) — _DEER_

○ What is the English for CHIEN? (SHEE AHn) — _DOG_

○ What is the English for VACHE? (VASH) — _COW_

○ What is the English for HERISSON? (AYREESO-n) — _HEDGEHOG_

○ What is the English for ANIMAL? (ANEEMAL) — _ANIMAL_

○ What is the English for CHEVAL? (SHeVAL)* — _HORSE_

○ What is the English for CHEVRE? (SHEVR) — _GOAT_

○ What is the English for CHAT? (SHA) — _CAT_

○ What is the English for LAPIN? (LAPAHn) — _RABBIT_

TURN BACK FOR THE ANSWERS

*Remember that a small 'e' in the pronunciation always sounds like the 'u' in curl.

ELEMENTARY GRAMMAR

All nouns in French are either MASCULINE or FEMININE, even though **they may never have been alive.**

Because you cannot tell whether a word is masculine or feminine just by listening to it, you will now be shown how to remember the gender of words in French.

If the word is MASCULINE, always associate it in your mind's eye with a boxer.

For example,

RABBIT is MASCULINE in French:

Imagine a boxer punching a rabbit.

Every time you see a word with a boxer, you will know that it is masculine.

If the word is FEMININE, always imagine the word interacting with a bottle of French perfume. For example,

COW is FEMININE in French.

Imagine a cow with a bottle of perfume dangling from her neck.

When you see a bottle of perfume in your mind's eye interacting with a word, you will know the word is feminine in French.

MASCULINE NOUNS

The French for THE when the noun is masculine is LE (pronounced Le).

For example,

THE DOG is LE CHIEN

THE CAT is LE CHAT

FEMININE NOUNS

The French for THE when the nouns is feminine is LA (pronounced LA).

For example,

THE COW   is LA VACHE

THE GOAT is LA CHEVRE

Imagine thinking "Ooh! La! La! what a beautiful cow".

PLURALS

If the French is plural, then the word for THE is always LES (pronounced LAY).

Finally, if a word starts with a vowel (like ANIMAL) then the word for THE is L' (for example, L'ANIMAL or L'OIE) no matter what the gender.

GENDERS

THINK OF EACH IMAGE IN YOUR MIND'S EYE FOR ABOUT TEN SECONDS

○ The gender of RABBIT is MASCULINE
   Imagine a boxer punching a rabbit.
              LE LAPIN

○ The gender of CAT is MASCULINE
   Imagine a boxer with a cat on his knee.
              LE CHAT

○ The gender of GOAT is FEMININE
   Imagine pouring a bottle of perfume over a goat to stop the smell.
              LA CHEVRE
              SHEEVRA.

○ The gender of HORSE is MASCULINE
   Imagine a boxer riding to the ring on a horse.
              LE CHEVAL

○ The gender of ANIMAL is MASCULINE
   Imagine a boxer in a ring surrounded by animals.
              L'ANIMAL

○ The gender of HEDGEHOG is MASCULINE
   Imagine a boxer sitting on a hedgehog.
              LE HERISSON

○ The gender of COW is FEMININE
   Imagine a cow with a bottle of perfume dangling from her neck instead of a bell.
              LA VACHE

○ The gender of DOG is MASCULINE
   Imagine a boxer dog with a boxer.
              LE CHIEN

○ The gender of DEER is MASCULINE
   Imagine a boxer with a deer slung over his shoulder.
              LE CERF

○ The gender of GOOSE is FEMININE
   Imagine a goose pecking at a bottle of perfume.
              L'OIE
              WA.

YOU CAN WRITE YOUR ANSWERS IN

F ○ What is the gender and French for goose?   *Un oie L'oie*

m ○ What is the gender and French for deer?   *Le cerf*

m ○ What is the gender and French for dog?   *Le chien*

F ○ What is the gender and French for cow?   *La vache*

m ○ What is the gender and French for hedgehog?   *Le herisson*

m ○ What is the gender and French for animal?   *L'animal*

m ○ What is the gender and French for horse?   *Le cheval*

F ○ What is the gender and French for goat?   ×   *Le chèvre*

m ○ What is the gender and French for cat?   *Le chat*

m ○ What is the gender and French for rabbit?   *Le lapin*

TURN BACK FOR THE ANSWERS

SOME MORE ANIMALS

THINK OF EACH IMAGE IN YOUR MIND'S EYE FOR ABOUT TEN SECONDS

○ The French for FISH is POISSON   (PWASOHn)
Imagine that you POISON your pet fish.

○ The French for TROUT is TRUITE   (TRWEET)
Imagine eating a beautiful trout —
a TRUE EAT.

○ The French for LOBSTER is HOMARD   (OMAR)
Imagine the famous actor OMAR Sharif eating
a huge lobster.

○ The French for SHEEP is MOUTON   (MOOTOHn)
Imagine getting MUTTON from a live sheep.

○ The French for MOUSE is SOURIS   (SOOREE)
Imagine a mouse running through a SEWER.

○ The French for OYSTER is HUITRE   (WEETR)
Imagine throwing an oyster into a WHEAT
field.

○ The French for WASP is GUEPE   (GEP)
Imagine a wasp flying through a GAP in a
wall.

○ The French for ELEPHANT is ELEPHANT   (AYLAYFOn)
Imagine an ELEPHANT climbing up the
Eiffel Tower.

○ The French for HEN is POULE   (POOL)
Imagine a hen in a POOL of water.

○ The French for DUCK is CANARD   (KANAR)
Imagine someone who cans dead ducks — a
duck CANNER.

YOU CAN WRITE YOUR ANSWERS IN

○ What is the English for CANARD?
(KANAR)

DUCK

○ What is the English for POULE? (POOL)

HEN

○ What is the English for ELEPHANT?
(AYLAYFOn)

ELEPHANT

○ What is the English for GUEPE? (GEP)

WASP

○ What is the English for HUITRE?
(WEETR)

OYSTER

○ What is the English for SOURIS?
(SOOREE)

MOUSE

○ What is the English for MOUTON?
(MOOTOHn)

SHEEP

○ What is the English for HOMARD?
(OMAR)

LOBSTER

○ What is the English for TRUITE?
(TRWEET)

TROUT

○ What is the English for POISSON?
(PWASOHn)

FISH.

TURN BACK FOR THE ANSWERS

GENDERS

THINK OF EACH IMAGE IN YOUR MIND'S EYE FOR ABOUT TEN SECONDS

○ The gender of FISH is MASCULINE   LE POISSON
Imagine a boxer fishing for fish.

○ The gender of TROUT is FEMININE   LA TRUITE
Imagine a trout cooked in a perfumed sauce.

○ The gender of LOBSTER is MASCULINE   LE HOMARD
Imagine a boxer tucking into a delicious meal of lobster.

○ The gender of SHEEP is MASCULINE   LE MOUTON
Imagine a boxer bringing his pet sheep into the ring.

○ The gender of MOUSE is FEMININE·   LA SOURIS
Imagine drowning a little mouse in a bottle of perfume.

○ The gender of OYSTER is FEMININE   L'HUITRE
Imagine oysters dipped in perfume before being swallowed.

○ The gender of WASP is FEMININE   LA GUEPE
Imagine wasps swarming around a bottle of perfume.

○ The gender of ELEPHANT is MASCULINE   L'ELEPHANT
Imagine a boxer riding on an elephant into the ring.

○ The gender of HEN is FEMININE   LA POULE*
Imagine a hen pecking at a bottle of perfume.

○ The gender of DUCK is MASCULINE   LE CANARD
Imagine a boxer shooing ducks out of the boxing ring.

* Note: CHICKEN is LE POULET

YOU CAN WRITE YOUR ANSWERS IN

○ What is the gender and French for duck? _____

○ What is the gender and French for hen? _____

○ What is the gender and French for elephant? _____

○ What is the gender and French for wasp? _____

○ What is the gender and French for oyster? _____

○ What is the gender and French for mouse? _____

○ What is the gender and French for sheep? _____

○ What is the gender and French for lobster? _____

○ What is the gender and French for trout? _____

○ What is the gender and French for fish? _____

TURN BACK FOR THE ANSWERS

This page will deal with some useful words which do not have any genders for you to remember.

THINK OF EACH IMAGE IN YOUR MIND'S EYE FOR ABOUT TEN SECONDS

○ The French for TIRED is FATIGUE   (FATEEGAY)
Imagine being TIRED and FATIGUED.

○ The French for QUICK is RAPIDE   (RAPEED)
Imagine being QUICK and RAPID.

○ The French for QUIET is TRANQUILLE   (TROnKEEL)
Imagine everything being QUIET and TRANQUIL.

○ The French for BIG is GRAND   (GROn)
Imagine something being BIG and GRAND.

○ The French for SMALL is PETIT   (PeTEE)
Imagine a PETITE LITTLE girl.

○ The French for HEAVY is LOURD   (LOOR)
Imagine you LURE a HEAVY man to his doom.

○ The French for THIN is MINCE   (MAHnS)
Imagine having a roMANCE with a THIN partner.

○ The French for DIRTY is SALE   (SAL)
Imagine eating a very DIRTY SALAD.

19

YOU CAN WRITE YOUR ANSWERS IN

○ What is the English for SALE? (SAL)   _____

○ What is the English for MINCE? (MAHnS)   _____

○ What is the English for LOURD? (LOOR)   _____

○ What is the English for PETIT? (PeTEE)   _____

○ What is the English for GRAND? (GROn)   _____

○ What is the English for TRANQUILLE?
(TROnKEEL)   _____

○ What is the English for RAPIDE?
(RAPEED)   _____

○ What is the English for FATIGUE?
(FATEEGAY)   _____

TURN BACK FOR THE ANSWERS

YOU CAN WRITE YOUR ANSWERS IN

○ What is the French for dirty? _____

○ What is the French for thin? _____

○ What is the French for heavy? _____

○ What is the French for small? _____

○ What is the French for big? _____

○ What is the French for quiet? _____

○ What is the French for quick? _____

○ What is the French for tired? _____

TURN BACK FOR THE ANSWERS

ELEMENTARY GRAMMAR

The French for IS is EST
(pronounced EH)

To say THE DOG IS QUICK
you simply say LE CHIEN EST RAPIDE

PLEASE NOTE:

EST is pronounced ET when it comes before a vowel.

Now cover up the answers below and translate the following:

(You can write your answers in)

1. THE HEDGEHOG IS SMALL
2. THE DEER IS TIRED
3. THE HORSE IS BIG
4. THE LOBSTER IS DIRTY
5. THE CAT IS HEAVY

The answers are:

1. LE HERISSON EST PETIT
2. LE CERF EST FATIGUE
3. LE CHEVAL EST GRAND
4. LE HOMARD EST SALE
5. LE CHAT EST LOURD

Now cover up the answers below and translate the following:

(You can write your answers in)

1. LA CHEVRE EST MINCE
2. L'HUITRE EST RAPIDE
3. LE MOUTON EST PETIT
4. L'ELEPHANT EST GRAND
5. LE CANARD EST SALE

The answers are:

1. THE GOAT IS THIN
2. THE OYSTER IS QUICK
3. THE SHEEP IS SMALL
4. THE ELEPHANT IS BIG
5. THE DUCK IS DIRTY

IMPORTANT NOTE

Some of the sentences in this course might strike you as being a bit odd!

However, they have been carefully constructed to make you think much more about what you are translating. This helps the memory process and gets away from the idea of learning useful phrases "parrot fashion".

But of course, having learned with the help of these seemingly odd sentences, you can easily construct your own sentences to suit your particular needs.

Section 2 HOTEL/HOME, FURNITURE, COLOURS

FURNITURE AND FITTINGS

THINK OF EACH IMAGE IN YOUR MIND'S EYE FOR ABOUT TEN SECONDS

○ The French for TABLE is TABLE   (TABL)
   Imagine throwing a TABLE from the top of the
   Eiffel Tower.

○ The French for CHAIR is CHAISE   (SHEZ)
   Imagine you have SHARES in a chair.

○ The French for CUPBOARD is PLACARD   (PLAKAR)
   Imagine a PLACARD stuck to a cupboard.

○ The French for WARDROBE is ARMOIRE   (ARMWAR)
   Imagine your ARM WORN out by trying to
   open a wardrobe door that is stuck.

○ The French for CLOCK is PENDULE   (POnDooL)
   Imagine a grandfather clock with a large PENDULUM.

○ The French for BED is LIT   (LEE)
   Imagine you LAY on a bed.

○ The French for PIANO is PIANO   (PEE ANOH)
   Imagine playing a PIANO at the top of the
   Eiffel Tower.

○ The French for CURTAIN is RIDEAU   (REEDOH)
   Imagine having to RE-DO the curtains after
   you have made a mess of them.

○ The French for ARMCHAIR is FAUTEUIL   (FOTOEY)
   Imagine taking a PHOTO of an armchair.

○ The French for CARPET is TAPIS   (TAPEE)
   Imagine your carpet with a TAPESTRY border.

YOU CAN WRITE YOUR ANSWERS IN

○ What is the English for TAPIS? (TAPEE) _____

○ What is the English for FAUTEUIL? (FOTOEY) _____

○ What is the English for RIDEAU? (REEDOH) _____

○ What is the English for PIANO? (PEE ANOH) _____

○ What is the English for LIT? (LEE) _____

○ What is the English for PENDULE? (POnDooL) _____

○ What is the English for ARMOIRE? (ARMWAR) _____

○ What is the English for PLACARD? (PLAKAR) _____

○ What is the English for CHAISE? (SHEZ) _____

○ What is the English for TABLE? (TABL) _____

TURN BACK FOR THE ANSWERS

THINK OF EACH IMAGE IN YOUR MIND'S EYE FOR ABOUT TEN SECONDS

○ The gender of TABLE is FEMININE   **LA TABLE**
  Imagine a large bottle of perfume on the table.

○ The gender of CHAIR is FEMININE   **LA CHAISE**
Imagine spilling perfume on a chair to make it smell better.

○ The gender of CUPBOARD is MASCULINE   **LE PLACARD**
Imagine a boxer punching a cupboard.

○ The gender of WARDROBE is FEMININE   **L'ARMOIRE**
Imagine spilling perfume onto your wardrobe to stop the smell of mothballs.

○ The gender of CLOCK is FEMININE   **LA PENDULE**
Imagine a bottle of perfume at the bottom of the pendulum of a clock.

○ The gender of BED is MASCULINE   **LE LIT**
Imagine putting a boxer to bed after a bad fight.

○ The gender of PIANO is MASCULINE   **LE PIANO**
Imagine a boxer trying to play the piano with boxing gloves on.

○ The gender of CURTAIN is MASCULINE   **LE RIDEAU**
Imagine a boxer climbing up a curtain.

○ The gender of ARMCHAIR is MASCULINE
Imagine a boxer slumped in your favourite   **LE FAUTEUIL**
armchair.

○ The gender of CARPET is MASCULINE   **LE TAPIS**
Imagine a carpeted boxing ring, with a boxer lying on the carpet.

YOU CAN WRITE YOUR ANSWERS IN

○ What is the gender and French for carpet? _____

○ What is the gender and French for armchair? _____

○ What is the gender and French for curtain? _____

○ What is the gender and French for piano? _____

○ What is the gender and French for bed? _____

○ What is the gender and French for clock? _____

○ What is the gender and French for wardrobe? _____

○ What is the gender and French for cupboard? _____

○ What is the gender and French for chair? _____

○ What is the gender and French for table? _____

TURN BACK FOR THE ANSWERS

SOME MORE HOUSE WORDS

THINK OF EACH IMAGE IN YOUR MIND'S EYE FOR ABOUT TEN SECONDS

○ The French for DOOR is PORTE　　　　　　　(PORT)
Imagine a PORT with a huge door at the
entrance.

○ The French for WINDOW is FENETRE　　　　(FeNETR)
Imagine covering windows with a FINE NET.

○ The French for GARDEN is JARDIN　　　　(JARDAHn)
Imagine a GARDEN on the top of the Eiffel
Tower.

○ The French for ROOF is TOIT　　　　　　　　(TWA)
Imagine a TWANging noise on the roof.

○ The French for CEILING is PLAFOND　　　(PLAFOHn)
Imagine using a PLATFORM to paint the
ceiling.

○ The French for STAIRCASE is ESCALIER　(ESKALEE AY)
Imagine your staircase is like an
ESCALATOR.

○ The French for FLOOR is PLANCHER　　　(PLOnSHAY)
Imagine PLUNGING through rotten floors.

○ The French for WALL is MUR　　　　　　　(MooR)
Imagine a MURAL painted on your wall.

○ The French for KITCHEN is CUISINE　　(KWEEZEEN)
Imagine preparing beautiful CUISINE in
your kitchen.

○ The French for ROOM is PIECE　　　　　　(PEE ES)
Imagine someone writing to you to say "P.S.
Your room will be very small."

YOU CAN WRITE YOUR ANSWERS IN

○ What is the English for PIECE? (PEE ES) _____

○ What is the English for CUISINE? (KWEEZEEN) _____

○ What is the English for MUR? (MooR) _____

○ What is the English for PLANCHER? (PLOnSHAY) _____

○ What is the English for ESCALIER? (ESKALEE AY) _____

○ What is the English for PLAFOND? (PLAFOHn) _____

○ What is the English for TOIT? (TWA) _____

○ What is the English for JARDIN? (JARDAHn) _____

○ What is the English for FENETRE? (FeNETR) _____

○ What is the English for PORTE? (PORT) _____

TURN BACK FOR THE ANSWERS

THINK OF EACH IMAGE IN YOUR MIND'S EYE FOR ABOUT TEN SECONDS

○ The gender of DOOR is FEMININE   LA PORTE
Imagine a bottle of perfume used as a door knocker on a door.

○ The gender of WINDOW is FEMININE   LA FENETRE
Imagine spraying a window with perfume and using it as a window cleaner.

○ The gender of GARDEN is MASCULINE   LE JARDIN
Imagine a boxing match in your garden.

○ The gender of ROOF is MASCULINE   LE TOIT
Imagine two boxers fighting on a roof.

○ The gender of CEILING is MASCULINE   LE PLAFOND
Imagine a boxer being punched so hard he bangs his head on the ceiling.

○ The gender of STAIRCASE is   L'ESCALIER
MASCULINE
Imagine a boxer falling down some stairs.

○ The gender of FLOOR is MASCULINE   LE PLANCHER
Imagine a boxer on the floor.

○ The gender of WALL is MASCULINE   LE MUR
Imagine a boxer sitting on a wall.

○ The gender of KITCHEN is FEMININE   LA CUISINE
Imagine spraying your kitchen with perfume to hide bad smells.

○ The gender of ROOM is FEMININE   LA PIECE
Imagine a room stacked full of bottles of perfume.

YOU CAN WRITE YOUR ANSWERS IN

○ What is the gender and French for room? _____

○ What is the gender and French for kitchen? _____

○ What is the gender and French for wall? _____

○ What is the gender and French for floor? _____

○ What is the gender and French for stairs? _____

○ What is the gender and French for ceiling? _____

○ What is the gender and French for roof? _____

○ What is the gender and French for garden? _____

○ What is the gender and French for window? _____

○ What is the gender and French for door? _____

TURN BACK FOR THE ANSWERS

COLOURS

THINK OF EACH IMAGE IN YOUR MIND'S EYE FOR ABOUT TEN SECONDS

○ The French for BLACK is NOIR   (NWAR)
Imagine someone telling you "There is NO 'R' in black."

○ The French for WHITE is BLANC   (BLOn)
Imagine a BLONDE, white-haired girl.

○ The French for RED is ROUGE   (ROOJ)
Imagine someone whose face is reddened with ROUGE.

○ The French for YELLOW is JAUNE   (JON)
Imagine someone yellow from JAUNDICE.

○ The French for GREEN is VERT   (VER)
Imagine someone with a VERY green face.

○ The French for BLUE is BLEU   (BLe)
Imagine painting the Eiffel Tower blue.

○ The French for PINK is ROSE   (ROZ)
Imagine a pink ROSE.

○ The French for ORANGE is ORANGE   (OROnJ)
Imagine painting the Eiffel Tower a bright orange.

○ The French for GOLD(en) is DORE   (DORAY)
Imagine a gold DOOR.

○ The French for GREY is GRIS   (GREE)
Imagine grey coloured GREASE.

YOU CAN WRITE YOUR ANSWERS IN

○ What is the English for GRIS? (GREE) _____

○ What is the English for DORE? (DORAY) _____

○ What is the English for ORANGE? (OROnJ) _____

○ What is the English for ROSE? (ROZ) _____

○ What is the English for BLEU? (BLe) _____

○ What is the English for VERT? (VER) _____

○ What is the English for JAUNE? (JON) _____

○ What is the English for ROUGE? (ROOJ) _____

○ What is the English for BLANC? (BLOn) _____

○ What is the English for NOIR? (NWAR) _____

TURN BACK FOR THE ANSWERS

YOU CAN WRITE YOUR ANSWERS IN

○ What is the French for grey? _____

○ What is the French for gold(en)? _____

○ What is the French for orange? _____

○ What is the French for pink? _____

○ What is the French for blue? _____

○ What is the French for green? _____

○ What is the French for yellow? _____

○ What is the French for red? _____

○ What is the French for white? _____

○ What is the French for black? _____

TURN BACK FOR THE ANSWERS

ELEMENTARY GRAMMAR

In French, adjectives (like BIG, DIRTY, etc.) change their endings to agree with the gender of the word they go with.

When the word is FEMININE, then you normally add an "e" to the end of the adjective.

For example,

PETIT CHIEN (masculine)	is	LITTLE DOG
PETITE CHEVRE (feminine)	is	LITTLE GOAT
GRAND TAPIS (masculine)	is	BIG CARPET
GRANDE TABLE (feminine)	is	BIG TABLE

In the MASCULINE, the last consonant is not normally pronounced.

So,

PETIT is pronounced PeTEE.

However, in the FEMININE, you do pronounce the last consonant.

So,

PETITE is pronounced PeTEET

Again, GRAND   is pronounced GROn

GRANDE is pronounced GROnD

If, however, the adjective already ends in "e" (for example RAPIDE, SALE, etc.) then you make no change in either spelling or pronunciation in the feminine.

PLEASE NOTE: The FEMININE of:
WHITE is BLANCHE (BLOnSH)
GREY   is GRISE (GREEZ)

Now cover up the answers below and translate the following:

(You can write your answers in)

1. THE CHAIR IS PINK
2. THE WARDROBE IS BLUE
3. THE CUPBOARD IS GREEN
4. THE BED IS HEAVY
5. THE GOOSE IS TIRED

The answers are:

1. LA CHAISE EST ROSE
2. L'ARMOIRE EST BLEUE
3. LE PLACARD EST VERT
4. LE LIT EST LOURD
5. L'OIE EST FATIGUEE

Now cover up the answers below and translate the following:

(You can write your answers in)

1. LE PIANO EST BLANC
2. LE TAPIS EST SALE
3. LE RIDEAU EST DORE
4. LE FAUTEUIL EST GRAND
5. L'ESCALIER EST LOURD

The answers are:

1. THE PIANO IS WHITE
2. THE CARPET IS DIRTY
3. THE CURTAIN IS GOLD(EN)
4. THE ARMCHAIR IS BIG
5. THE STAIRCASE IS HEAVY

SOME USEFUL WORDS FOR MAKING SENTENCES

THINK OF EACH IMAGE IN YOUR MIND'S EYE FOR ABOUT TEN SECONDS

○ The French for EATS is MANGE   (MOnJ)*
   Imagine EATing blancMANGE.

○ The French for HAS is A   (A)
   Imagine someone HAS A something or other.

○ The French for WANTS is VEUT   (Ve)
   Imagine you WANT a FUR coat.

○ The French for SEES is VOIT   (VWA)
   Imagine a German saying "I SEE VWATER in the
   sea."

*Remember that a 'J' in the pronunciation always sounds like the 's' in pleasure.

YOU CAN WRITE YOUR ANSWERS IN

○ What is the English for VOIT? (VWA) _____

○ What is the English for VEUT? (Ve) _____

○ What is the English for A? (A) _____

○ What is the English for MANGE? (MOnJ) _____

TURN BACK FOR THE ANSWERS

YOU CAN WRITE YOUR ANSWERS IN

○ What is the French for sees?   _____

○ What is the French for wants?   _____

○ What is the French for has?   _____

○ What is the French for eats?   _____

TURN BACK FOR THE ANSWERS

ELEMENTARY GRAMMAR

Adjectives in French often come after the noun.

For example,

BLACK DOG is CHIEN NOIR

QUICK CAT is CHAT RAPIDE

With one or two exceptions, it is not wrong to put the adjectives you have already been given after the noun.

For example,

RED TABLE is TABLE ROUGE

QUIET COW is VACHE TRANQUILLE

The two exceptions of the words you have just learnt are:

BIG   — GRAND

SMALL — PETIT

which almost always come BEFORE the noun.

For example,

BIG RABBIT   is GRAND LAPIN

SMALL CHAIR is PETITE CHAISE

Now cover up the answers below and translate the following:

(You can write your answers in)

1. THE BLACK HORSE EATS THE GREEN CHAIR
2. THE LITTLE MOUSE SEES THE BIG DEER
3. THE QUICK TROUT HAS THE RED LOBSTER
4. THE TIRED ANIMAL WANTS THE GREY BED
5. THE YELLOW CLOCK IS BIG

The answers are:

1. LE CHEVAL NOIR MANGE LA CHAISE VERTE
2. LA PETITE SOURIS VOIT LE GRAND CERF
3. LA TRUITE RAPIDE A LE HOMARD ROUGE
4. L'ANIMAL FATIGUE VEUT LE LIT GRIS
5. LA PENDULE JAUNE EST GRANDE

Now cover up the answers below and translate the following:

(You can write your answers in)

1. LA PETITE VACHE VOIT LA PORTE NOIRE
2. LE MUR VERT EST SALE
3. LA CHEVRE FATIGUEE VEUT LA FENETRE BLEUE
4. L'OIE RAPIDE MANGE LE TOIT ORANGE
5. LE CHAT NOIR A LE PLANCHER ROUGE

The answers are:

1. THE LITTLE COW SEES THE BLACK DOOR
2. THE GREEN WALL IS DIRTY
3. THE TIRED GOAT WANTS THE BLUE WINDOW
4. THE QUICK GOOSE EATS THE ORANGE ROOF
5. THE BLACK CAT HAS THE RED FLOOR

Section 3 CLOTHES/FAMILY WORDS

CLOTHES

THINK OF EACH IMAGE IN YOUR MIND'S EYE FOR ABOUT TEN SECONDS

○ The French for CLOTHES is VETEMENTS (VETMOn)
Imagine that you explain to your mother "I took all my clothes to the VET MA."

○ The French for UNDERPANTS is SLIP (SLEEP)
Imagine you SLEEP in your underpants.

○ The French for TROUSERS is PANTALON (POnTALOHn)
Imagine your trousers are baggy PANTALOONS.

○ The French for SKIRT is JUPE (JooP)
Imagine spilling SOUP on your skirt.

○ The French for SOCK is CHAUSSETTE (SHOSET)
Imagine you buy a magnificent pair of socks — they are a SHOW SET.

○ The French for JACKET is VESTE (VEST)
Imagine you wear a VEST while everybody· else is wearing a smart jacket to a dance.

○ The French for DRESS is ROBE (ROB)
Imagine someone ROBS you of your best dress.

○ The French for PULLOVER is PULLOVER (PooLOVER)
Imagine taking your PULLOVER off at the top of the Eiffel Tower.

○ The French for SHOE is CHAUSSURE (SHOSooR)
Imagine Geoffrey CHAUCER, the author of *The Canterbury Tales*, trying on a shoe on his way to Canterbury.

○ The French for HAT is CHAPEAU (SHAPOH)
Imagine taking off your hat when you enter a CHAPEL.

YOU CAN WRITE YOUR ANSWERS IN

○ What is the English for CHAPEAU?
(SHAPOH) _____

○ What is the English for CHAUSSURE?
(SHOSooR) _____

○ What is the English for PULLOVER?
(PooLOVER) _____

○ What is the English for ROBE? (ROB) _____

○ What is the English for VESTE? (VEST) _____

○ What is the English for CHAUSSETTE?
(SHOSET) _____

○ What is the English for JUPE? (JooP) _____

○ What is the English for PANTALON?
(POnTALOHn) _____

○ What is the English for SLIP? (SLEEP) _____

○ What is the English for VETEMENTS?
(VETMOn) _____

TURN BACK FOR THE ANSWERS

THINK OF EACH IMAGE IN YOUR MIND'S EYE FOR ABOUT TEN SECONDS

○ The gender of VETEMENTS is **LES VETEMENTS**
MASCULINE
Imagine a boxer putting clothes on after a fight.
(N.B. This is a plural word. The word for
THE in the plural is LES.)

○ The gender of UNDERPANTS is MASCULINE **LE SLIP**
Imagine a boxer fighting in his underpants.

○ The gender of TROUSERS is **LE PANTALON**
MASCULINE
Imagine a boxer pulling on his trousers
after a fight.

○ The gender of SKIRT is FEMININE **LA JUPE**
Imagine spilling perfume on a skirt.

○ The gender of SOCK is FEMININE **LA CHAUSSETTE**
Imagine spraying perfume on your socks
to kill the smell.

○ The gender of JACKET is FEMININE **LA VESTE**
Imagine spraying your jacket with
perfume to make it smell nice.

○ The gender of DRESS is FEMININE **LA ROBE**
Imagine spilling a bottle of perfume all
over a dress.

○ The gender of PULLOVER is **LE PULLOVER**
MASCULINE
Imagine a boxer wearing a pullover
during a fight.

○ The gender of SHOE is FEMININE **LA CHAUSSURE**
Imagine spraying the uppers of your
shoe with perfume to improve the smell.

○ The gender of HAT is MASCULINE **LE CHAPEAU**
Imagine a boxer having a hat knocked off
his head in a fight.

YOU CAN WRITE YOUR ANSWERS IN

○ What is the gender and French for hat? _____

○ What is the gender and French for shoe? _____

○ What is the gender and French for pullover? _____

○ What is the gender and French for dress? _____

○ What is the gender and French for jacket? _____

○ What is the gender and French for sock? _____

○ What is the gender and French for skirt? _____

○ What is the gender and French for trousers? _____

○ What is the gender and French for underpants? _____

○ What is the gender and French for clothes? _____

TURN BACK FOR THE ANSWERS

50

ELEMENTARY GRAMMAR

The French word for I is JE (pronounced Je)

The French word for AM is SUIS (pronounced SWEE)

Imagine I AM a SWEDE.

To say   I AM (e.g. I AM THE DOG)
you say JE SUIS LE CHIEN
To say   I AM THE DOOR
you say JE SUIS LA PORTE

The French word for HE is IL (pronounced EEL)

Imagine HE is in an EEL.

So,

HE IS   is IL EST
HE EATS   is IL MANGE
HE IS TIRED is IL EST FATIGUE

The French word for SHE is ELLE (pronounced EL)

Imagine SHE is HELL to live with.

So,

SHE SEES   is ELLE VOIT
SHE IS DIRTY is ELLE EST SALE

Now translate the following:

(You can write your answers in)

1. HE SEES THE BLUE JACKET
2. I AM THE BIG CAT
3. SHE HAS THE HEAVY PULLOVER
4. HE WANTS THE YELLOW SOCK
5. SHE EATS THE RED SHOE

The answers are:

1. IL VOIT LA VESTE BLEUE
2. JE SUIS LE GRAND CHAT
3. ELLE A LE PULLOVER LOURD
4. IL VEUT LA CHAUSSETTE JAUNE
5. ELLE MANGE LA CHAUSSURE ROUGE

Now cover up the answers below and translate the following:

(You can write your answers in)

1. IL VOIT LE PLAFOND ROSE
2. ELLE VEUT LA JUPE SALE
3. JE SUIS L'ANIMAL NOIR
4. IL MANGE LA ROBE GRISE
5. ELLE A LES VETEMENTS JAUNES

PLEASE NOTE that with this last sentence you add an "s" to the adjective.

This will be dealt with more fully later on.

The answers are:

1. HE SEES THE PINK CEILING
2. SHE WANTS THE DIRTY SKIRT
3. I AM THE BLACK ANIMAL
4. HE EATS THE GREY DRESS
5. SHE HAS THE YELLOW CLOTHES

FAMILY WORDS

THINK OF EACH IMAGE IN YOUR MIND'S EYE FOR ABOUT TEN SECONDS

○ The French for FATHER is PERE   (PER)
Imagine your father eating a PEAR.

○ The French for MOTHER is MERE   (MER)
Imagine your mother mounted on a grey MARE.

○ The French for BROTHER is FRERE   (FRER)
Imagine your brother dressed up as a holy FRIAR.

○ The French for SISTER is SOEUR   (SeR)
Imagine your sister saying "Hello SIR".

○ The French for HUSBAND is MARI   (MAREE)
Imagine you MARRY your husband.

○ The French for WIFE is FEMME   (FAM)
Imagine men eating their wives in a FAMine.
(N.B. FEMME is the same as the word for WOMAN).

○ The French for SON is FILS   (FEES)
Imagine having to pay school FEES for your son.

○ The French for DAUGHTER is FILLE   (FEE)
Imagine selling your daughter for a FEE.

○ The French for BOY is GARÇON   (GARSOHn)
Imagine a young boy has left the GAS ON.
(N.B. GARÇON is the same as the word for
WAITER).

○ The French for GIRL is JEUNE FILLE   (JeN FEE)
Imagine a girl on a YOUNG FILLY.

YOU CAN WRITE YOUR ANSWERS IN

○ What is the English for JEUNE FILLE?
  (JeN FEE) _____

○ What is the English for GARÇON?
  (GARSOHn) _____

○ What is the English for FILLE? (FEE) _____

○ What is the English for FILS? (FEES) _____

○ What is the English for FEMME? (FAM) _____

○ What is the English for MARI? (MAREE) _____

○ What is the English for SOEUR? (SeR) _____

○ What is the English for FRERE? (FRER) _____

○ What is the English for MERE? (MER) _____

○ What is the English for PERE? (PER) _____

TURN BACK FOR THE ANSWERS

YOU CAN WRITE YOUR ANSWERS IN

The genders of family words are given by the sex of the person.

○ What is the gender and French for girl?　　　＿＿＿＿＿＿＿＿

○ What is the gender and French for boy?　　　＿＿＿＿＿＿＿＿

○ What is the gender and French for
daughter?　　　　　　　　　　　　　　　＿＿＿＿＿＿＿＿

○ What is the gender and French for son?　　　＿＿＿＿＿＿＿＿

○ What is the gender and French for wife?　　＿＿＿＿＿＿＿＿

○ What is the gender and French for
husband?　　　　　　　　　　　　　　　　＿＿＿＿＿＿＿＿

○ What is the gender and French for sister?　　＿＿＿＿＿＿＿＿

○ What is the gender and French for brother?　＿＿＿＿＿＿＿＿

○ What is the gender and French for mother?　＿＿＿＿＿＿＿＿

○ What is the gender and French for father?　　＿＿＿＿＿＿＿＿

TURN BACK FOR THE ANSWERS

SOME MORE USEFUL WORDS

THINK OF EACH IMAGE IN YOUR MIND'S EYE FOR ABOUT TEN SECONDS

○ The French for EMPTY is VIDE   (VEED)
Imagine a German putting a VEED (weed) into
an EMPTY jar.

○ The French for DEEP is PROFOND   (PROFOHn)
Imagine thinking DEEP, PROFOUND thoughts.

○ The French for UGLY is LAID   (LAY)
Imagine an UGLY duckling LAYing an egg.

○ The French for EXPENSIVE is CHER   (SHER)
Imagine you SHARE the cost of an
EXPENSIVE meal.

○ The French for COLD is FROID   (FRWA)
Imagine you FRY a COLD sausage.

○ The French for HOT is CHAUD   (SHOH)
Imagine you try hard not to SHOW how HOT
you are.

○ The French for PRETTY is JOLI   (JOLEE)
Imagine a JOLLY, PRETTY girl.

YOU CAN WRITE YOUR ANSWERS IN

○ What is the English for JOLI? (JOLEE) _____

○ What is the English for CHAUD? (SHOH) _____

○ What is the English for FROID? (FRWA) _____

○ What is the English for CHER? (SHER) _____

○ What is the English for LAID? (LAY) _____

○ What is the English for PROFOUND?
(PROFOHn) _____

○ What is the English for VIDE? (VEED) _____

TURN BACK FOR THE ANSWERS

YOU CAN WRITE YOUR ANSWERS IN

○ What is the French for pretty?   _____

○ What is the French for hot?   _____

○ What is the French for cold?   _____

○ What is the French for expensive?   _____

○ What is the French for ugly?   _____

○ What is the French for deep?   _____

○ What is the French for empty?   _____

TURN BACK FOR THE ANSWERS

ELEMENTARY GRAMMAR
The French for AND is ET (pronounced AY like AID)

Imagine A AND b.

So,

HOT AND COLD   is CHAUD ET FROID
RED AND GREEN is ROUGE ET VERT

The French for BUT is MAIS (pronounced MAY)

Imagine you like any month BUT MAY.

So,

PRETTY BUT EXPENSIVE is JOLI MAIS CHER
SMALL BUT QUIET   is PETIT MAIS
                                      TRANQUILLE

The French for OR is OU (pronounced OO)

Imagine people say "OOH! OR AH!"

So,

THE DOG OR THE CAT   is LE CHIEN OU LE CHAT
THE WALL OR THE FLOOR   is LE MUR OU LE
                                       PLANCHER

Now cover up the answers below and translate the following:

(You can write your answers in)

1. HE EATS THE RABBIT AND THE HEDGEHOG
2. SHE WANTS THE KITCHEN OR THE GARDEN
3. I AM SMALL BUT HEAVY
4. SHE IS QUIET AND THIN, BUT PRETTY
5. THE ROOM IS EMPTY AND THE KITCHEN IS BLACK

The answers are:

1. IL MANGE LE LAPIN ET LE HERISSON
2. ELLE VEUT LA CUISINE OU LE JARDIN
3. JE SUIS PETIT MAIS LOURD
4. ELLE EST TRANQUILLE ET MINCE, MAIS JOLIE
5. LA PIECE EST VIDE ET LA CUISINE EST NOIRE

Now cover up the answers below and translate the following:

(You can write your answers in)

1. IL EST LE PERE ET ELLE EST LA MERE
2. JE SUIS LE FRERE SALE, MAIS LA SOEUR EST LOURDE
3. LA JEUNE FILLE MANGE LE GRAND FILS
4. IL VEUT LE JOLI MARI OU LA FEMME LAIDE
   (N.B. JOLI normally comes before the noun).
5. LE PERE EST LAID ET LA MERE EST GRANDE

The answers are:

1. HE IS THE FATHER AND SHE IS THE MOTHER
2. I AM THE DIRTY BROTHER, BUT THE SISTER IS HEAVY
3. THE GIRL EATS THE BIG SON
4. HE WANTS THE PRETTY HUSBAND OR THE UGLY WIFE
5. THE FATHER IS UGLY AND THE MOTHER IS BIG

Section 4   IN THE COUNTRY/TIME WORDS, NUMBERS

TRAVELLING IN THE COUNTRY

THINK OF EACH IMAGE IN YOUR MIND'S EYE FOR ABOUT TEN SECONDS

○ The French for GRASS is HERBE   (ERB)
   Imagine you use grass as a HERB to cure your
   sore leg.

○ The French for FLOWER is FLEUR   (FLeR)
   Imagine throwing FLOWERS from the top of
   the Eiffel Tower.

○ The French for TREE is ARBRE   (ARBR)
   Imagine a tree-lined HARBOUR.

○ The French for FRUIT is FRUIT   (FRWEE)
   Imagine getting some FREE fruit.

○ The French for FLY is MOUCHE   (MOOSH)
   Imagine you catch flies and MUSH them up.

○ The French for INSECT is INSECTE   (AHnSEKT)
   Imagine an INSECT crawling up
   the Eiffel Tower.

YOU CAN WRITE YOUR ANSWERS IN

○ What is the English for INSECTE?
(AHnSEKT) _____

○ What is the English for MOUCHE?
(MOOSH) _____

○ What is the English for FRUIT? (FRWEE) _____

○ What is the English for ARBRE? (ARBR) _____

○ What is the English for FLEUR? (FLeR) _____

○ What is the English for HERBE? (ERB) _____

TURN BACK FOR THE ANSWERS

THINK OF EACH IMAGE IN YOUR MIND'S EYE FOR ABOUT TEN SECONDS

○ The gender of HERBE is FEMININE   L'HERBE
  Imagine spraying grass with perfume.

○ The gender of FLOWER is FEMININE   LA FLEUR
  Imagine making flowers into perfume.

○ The gender of TREE is MASCULINE   L'ARBRE
  Imagine a boxer using a tree as a punch bag.

○ The gender of FRUIT is MASCULINE   LE FRUIT
  Imagine a boxer eating a bag of fruit just
  before he gets up to fight.

○ The gender of FLY is FEMININE   LA MOUCHE
  Imagine spraying flies with a deadly perfume.

○ The gender of INSECT is MASCULINE   L'INSECTE
  Imagine a boxer stamping on all sorts of
  insects in the ring.

YOU CAN WRITE YOUR ANSWERS IN

○ What is the gender and French for insect?   _____

○ What is the gender and French for fly?   _____

○ What is the gender and French for fruit?   _____

○ What is the gender and French for tree?   _____

○ What is the gender and French for flower?   _____

○ What is the gender and French for grass?   _____

TURN BACK FOR THE ANSWERS

ELEMENTARY GRAMMAR

If you want to say A DOG, A BED, etc., then the word for "A" is UN

(pronounced en, something like the English 'earn'.)

So,

  A DOG is UN CHIEN

  A BED is UN LIT

For feminine words like A COW, A FLOWER, etc., the word for "A" is UNE

(pronounced ooN).

So,

  A COW   is UNE VACHE

  A FLOWER is UNE FLEUR

Now cover up the answers below and translate the following:

(You can write the answers in)

1. HE HAS A DOG AND HE WANTS A TREE
2. A GOAT IS BLACK BUT A FRUIT IS RED
3. A FISH EATS A WASP
4. THE WINDOW IS BLUE BUT THE GRASS IS GREEN
5. AN INSECT IS SMALL BUT A FLY IS BIG

The answers are:

1. IL A UN CHIEN ET IL VEUT UN ARBRE
2. UNE CHEVRE EST NOIRE MAIS UN FRUIT EST ROUGE
3. UN POISSON MANGE UNE GUEPE
4. LA FENETRE EST BLEUE MAIS L'HERBE EST VERTE
5. UN INSECTE EST PETIT MAIS UNE MOUCHE EST GRANDE

Now cover up the answers below and translate the following:

(You can write the answers in)

1. UNE VACHE EST PETITE ET UN INSECTE EST GRAND
2. IL EST GRAND ET ELLE EST PETITE
3. IL MANGE UN CANARD BLEU, MAIS ELLE MANGE UNE OIE ROUGE
4. IL VOIT UNE TABLE ROSE, OU UNE TABLE VERTE
5. ELLE A UN RIDEAU BLEU ET UN PLACARD BLANC

The answers are:

1. A COW IS SMALL AND AN INSECT IS BIG
2. HE IS BIG AND SHE IS SMALL
3. HE EATS A BLUE DUCK, BUT SHE EATS A RED GOOSE
4. HE SEES A PINK TABLE, OR A GREEN TABLE
5. SHE HAS A BLUE CURTAIN AND A WHITE CUPBOARD

TIME

THINK OF EACH IMAGE IN YOUR MIND'S EYE FOR ABOUT TEN SECONDS

○ The French for TIME is TEMPS   (TOn)
   Imagine keeping time with your TONGUE.

○ The French for SECOND is SECONDE   (SeGOHnD)
   Imagine seeing the Eiffel Tower for a split
   SECOND.

○ The French for MINUTE is MINUTE   (MEENooT)
   Imagine it takes you exactly one MINUTE to
   run to the top of the Eiffel Tower.

○ The French for HOUR is HEURE   (eR)
   Imagine you meet HER every hour.

○ The French for DAY is JOUR   (JOOR)
   Imagine not being SURE what day it is.

○ The French for WEEK is SEMAINE   (SeMEN)
   Imagine getting a SERMON from a priest once
   a week.

○ The French for MONTH is MOIS   (MWA)
   Imagine your MA gives you pocket money once
   a month.

○ The French for YEAR is AN   (On)
   Imagine thinking "OH! What a year!"

○ The French for MORNING is MATIN   (MATAHn)
   Imagine going to a theatre MATINEE in the
   morning.

○ The French for NIGHT is NUIT   (NWEE)
   Imagine thinking "It would be night wheN WE
   arrived home."

YOU CAN WRITE YOUR ANSWERS IN

○ What is the English for NUIT? (NWEE)　　　＿＿＿＿＿＿

○ What is the English for MATIN?
　(MATAHn)　　　　　　　　　　　　　　＿＿＿＿＿＿

○ What is the English for AN? (On)　　　　　＿＿＿＿＿＿

○ What is the English for MOIS? (MWA)　　　＿＿＿＿＿＿

○ What is the English for SEMAINE?
　(SeMEN)　　　　　　　　　　　　　　　＿＿＿＿＿＿

○ What is the English for JOUR? (JOOR)　　　＿＿＿＿＿＿

○ What is the English for HEURE? (eR)　　　＿＿＿＿＿＿

○ What is the English for MINUTE?
　(MEENooT)　　　　　　　　　　　　　＿＿＿＿＿＿

○ What is the English for SECONDE?
　(SeGOHnD)　　　　　　　　　　　　　＿＿＿＿＿＿

○ What is the English for TEMPS? (TOn)　　　＿＿＿＿＿＿

TURN BACK FOR THE ANSWERS

THINK OF EACH IMAGE IN YOUR MIND'S EYE FOR ABOUT TEN SECONDS

○ The gender of TIME is MASCULINE   LE TEMPS
Imagine a boxer looking anxiously at the
time to see when his fight starts.

○ The gender of SECOND is FEMININE   LA SECONDE
Imagine squirting perfume in short bursts of
1 second each.

○ The gender of MINUTE is FEMININE   LA MINUTE
Imagine bottles of perfume being sold from a
shop counter at a rate of one a minute.

○ The gender of HOUR is FEMININE   L'HEURE
Imagine lying in a bath of perfume for one hour.

○ The gender of DAY is MASCULINE   LE JOUR
Imagine a boxer who has a fight a day.

○ The gender of WEEK is FEMININE   LA SEMAINE
Imagine giving a bottle of perfume to your
mother once a week as a present.

○ The gender of MONTH is MASCULINE   LE MOIS
Imagine a boxer knocked out for a month.

○ The gender of YEAR is MASCULINE   L'AN
Imagine a boxer defending his title once a year.

○ The gender of MORNING is MASCULINE   LE MATIN
Imagine a boxer getting up early in the
morning to do his training.

○ The gender of NIGHT is FEMININE   LA NUIT
Imagine a beautiful still night filled with
fragrant perfume.

YOU CAN WRITE YOUR ANSWERS IN

○ What is the gender and French for night? _____

○ What is the gender and French for morning? _____

○ What is the gender and French for year? _____

○ What is the gender and French for month? _____

○ What is the gender and French for week? _____

○ What is the gender and French for day? _____

○ What is the gender and French for hour? _____

○ What is the gender and French for minute? _____

○ What is the gender and French for second? _____

○ What is the gender and French for time? _____

TURN BACK FOR THE ANSWERS

ELEMENTARY GRAMMAR

In French you normally make a word plural by adding an "s" at the end, but usually this is not pronounced.

For example, skirt (JUPE) becomes skirts (JUPES) and both are pronounced in the same way.

(pronounced just as the word JUPE).

The word for THE in the plural is LES — for both masculine and feminine words.

So,

THE SKIRTS	is	LES JUPES
THE DOGS	is	LES CHIENS
THE BLACK DOGS	is	LES CHIENS NOIRS

Note that you normally also add an "s" to the end of the adjective, but this is not pronounced either.

PLEASE NOTE that if you have a masculine and a feminine noun together like

THE DOG AND THE COW ARE SMALL

then "small" is used in a masculine way — i.e. PETITS.

In other words the masculine dominates the feminine.

The French for ARE in the sentence THE DOG AND THE CAT *ARE* BLACK is SONT

(pronounced SOHn).

So,

THE DOG AND THE CAT ARE BLACK

is LE CHIEN ET LE CHAT SONT NOIRS

Now translate the following:

(You can write your answers in)

1. THE GRASS AND THE TREE ARE GREEN
2. THE MONTH AND THE YEAR ARE QUIET
3. THE HEN AND THE WASP ARE QUICK BUT QUIET
4. THE INSECT AND THE FLY ARE DIRTY AND BIG
5. THE UNDERPANTS AND THE SOCK ARE RED AND GREEN
6. THE FLOWERS AND THE WASPS ARE SMALL
7. THE DIRTY SOCKS AND THE TROUSERS ARE PRETTY
8. THE BLACK SHOES AND THE GREEN PULLOVERS ARE EMPTY
9. THE HATS AND THE JACKETS ARE HEAVY AND RED
10. THE COLD KITCHEN AND THE BIG GARDEN ARE EMPTY AND UGLY

The answers are:

1. L'HERBE ET L'ARBRE SONT VERTS
2. LE MOIS ET L'AN SONT TRANQUILLES
3. LA POULE ET LA GUEPE SONT RAPIDES MAIS TRANQUILLES
4. L'INSECTE ET LA MOUCHE SONT SALES ET GRANDS
5. LE SLIP ET LA CHAUSSETTE SONT ROUGES ET VERTS
6. LES FLEURS ET LES GUEPES SONT PETITES
7. LES CHAUSSETTES SALES ET LE PANTALON SONT JOLIS
8. LES CHAUSSURES NOIRES ET LES PULLOVERS VERTS SONT VIDES
9. LES CHAPEAUX ET LES VESTES SONT LOURDS ET ROUGES
   (Note: a few words end with an "x" not an "s" in the plural).
10. LA CUISINE FROIDE ET LE GRAND JARDIN SONT VIDES ET LAIDS

Now translate the following:

(You can write your answers in)

1. LE CHIEN ET LE FRUIT SONT NOIRS
2. L'HEURE ET LE JOUR SONT TRANQUILLES ET GRIS
3. LE MATIN ET LA NUIT SONT NOIRS
4. LA SEMAINE EST TRANQUILLE, ET LA SECONDE ET LA MINUTE SONT TRANQUILLES
5. UNE FLEUR ET UN TOIT SONT VERTS
6. LES LAPINS ET LES CHATS SONT PETITS
7. LES VACHES OU LES TRUITES SONT GRANDES
8. LES TABLES ET LES CHIENS SONT LOURDS
9. LES ARMOIRES ET LES CHAISES SONT BLANCHES
10. LES CHAPEAUX ET LES ROBES SONT JOLIS MAIS CHERS

The answers are:

1. THE DOG AND THE FRUIT ARE BLACK
2. THE HOUR AND THE DAY ARE QUIET AND GREY
3. THE MORNING AND THE NIGHT ARE BLACK
4. THE WEEK IS QUIET, AND THE SECOND AND THE MINUTE ARE QUIET
5. A FLOWER AND A ROOF ARE GREEN
6. THE RABBITS AND THE CATS ARE SMALL
2. THE COWS OR THE TROUT ARE BIG
3. THE TABLES AND THE DOGS ARE HEAVY
4. THE WARDROBES AND THE CHAIRS ARE WHITE
10. THE HATS AND THE DRESSES ARE PRETTY BUT EXPENSIVE

NUMBERS

THINK OF EACH IMAGE IN YOUR MIND'S EYE FOR ABOUT TEN SECONDS

○ The French for ONE is UN   (en)
Imagine eating ONE ONion.

○ The French for TWO is DEUX   (De)
Imagine thinking "TWO will DO."

○ The French for THREE is TROIS   (TRWA)
Imagine you TRY to say trois THREE times.

○ The French for FOUR is QUATRE   (KATR)
Imagine looking at FOUR CATS.

○ The French for FIVE is CINQ   (SAHnK)
Imagine watching as FIVE ships SANK.

○ The French for SIX is SIX   (SEES)
Imagine telling someone to CEASE saying "SIX times SIX".

○ The French for SEVEN is SEPT   (SET)
Imagine you SET your alarm for SEVEN o'clock.

○ The French for EIGHT is HUIT   (WEET)
Imagine EIGHT sheaves of WHEAT.

○ The French for NINE is NEUF   (NeF)
Imagine saying "ENOUGH is enough. I'm going to dial 999."

○ The French for ZERO is ZERO   (ZAYROH)
Imagine meeting someone at the Eiffel Tower at ZERO hour.

PLEASE NOTE:

Numbers do not vary their endings, so they do not add an "s" in the plural.

YOU CAN WRITE YOUR ANSWERS IN

○ What is the English for ZERO? (ZAYROH)   _____

○ What is the English for NEUF? (NeF)   _____

○ What is the English for HUIT? (WEET)   _____

○ What is the English for SEPT? (SET)   _____

○ What is the English for SIX? (SEES)   _____

○ What is the English for CINQ? (SAHnK)   _____

○ What is the English for QUATRE? (KATR)   _____

○ What is the English for TROIS? (TRWA)   _____

○ What is the English for DEUX? (De)   _____

○ What is the English for UN? (en)   _____

TURN BACK FOR THE ANSWERS

YOU CAN WRITE YOUR ANSWERS IN

○ What is the French for zero?   _____

○ What is the French for nine?   _____

○ What is the French for eight?   _____

○ What is the French for seven?   _____

○ What is the French for six?   _____

○ What is the French for five?   _____

○ What is the French for four?   _____

○ What is the French for three?   _____

○ What is the French for two?   _____

○ What is the French for one?   _____

TURN BACK FOR THE ANSWERS

Now cover up the answers below and translate the following:

(You can write your answers in)

1. TWO FLOWERS ARE RED
2. FOUR RABBITS ARE THIN
3. FIVE INSECTS AND THREE FLIES ARE PRETTY
4. SEVEN TREES AND NINE DRESSES ARE EXPENSIVE
5. EIGHT SKIRTS ARE WHITE AND THREE DRESSES ARE GREEN

The answers are:

1. DEUX FLEURS SONT ROUGES
2. QUATRE LAPINS SONT MINCES
3. CINQ INSECTES ET TROIS MOUCHES SONT JOLIS
4. SEPT ARBRES ET NEUF ROBES SONT CHERS
5. HUIT JUPES SONT BLANCHES ET TROIS ROBES SONT VERTES

Now cover up the answers below and translate the following:

(You can write your answers in)

1. DEUX PULLOVERS SONT LAIDS
2. QUATRE POISSONS SONT CHERS
3. SIX FILS ET SEPT FILLES SONT SALES
4. NEUF MOUCHES ET HUIT GUEPES SONT NOIRES
5. TROIS FLEURS ET SEPT MURS SONT ROUGES

The answers are:

1. TWO PULLOVERS ARE UGLY
2. FOUR FISH ARE EXPENSIVE
3. SIX SONS AND SEVEN DAUGHTERS ARE DIRTY
4. NINE FLIES AND EIGHT WASPS ARE BLACK
5. THREE FLOWERS AND SEVEN WALLS ARE RED

Section 5 IN THE RESTAURANT, TELLING THE TIME

IN THE RESTAURANT

THINK OF EACH IMAGE IN YOUR MIND'S EYE FOR ABOUT TEN SECONDS

○ The French for RESTAURANT is   (RESTOROn)
   RESTAURANT
   Imagine a RESTAURANT at the top of
   the Eiffel Tower.

○ The French for KNIFE is COUTEAU   (KOOTOH)
   Imagine someone who tries to CUT YOU
   with a knife.

○ The French for FORK is FOURCHETTE   (FOORSHET)
   Imagine taking a fork and trying to
   FORCE IT through a door.

○ The French for SPOON is CUILLER   (KWEE ER)
   Imagine a QUEER shaped spoon.

○ The French for MENU is CARTE   (KART)
   Imagine a CART loaded to the top with menus.

○ The French for BILL is ADDITION   (ADEESEE OHn)
   Imagine practising your ADDITION as
   you add up a bill.

○ The French for WAITER is GARÇON   (GARSOHn)
   Imagine a waiter who has left the GAS ON,
   and burnt your meal.
   (N.B. GARÇON is the same as the word for BOY).

○ The French for WAITRESS is SERVEUSE   (SERVeZ)
   Imagine demanding that the waitress
   gives you SERVICE.

○ The French for CUP is TASSE   (TAS)
   Imagine a TASSLE hanging from the
   handle of a cup.

○ The French for PLATE is ASSIETTE   (ASEE ET)
   Imagine looking for a plate and saying
   "I SEE IT."

YOU CAN WRITE YOUR ANSWERS IN

○ What is the English for ASSIETTE?
(ASEE ET) _____

○ What is the English for TASSE? (TAS) _____

○ What is the English for SERVEUSE?
(SERVeZ) _____

○ What is the English for GARÇON?
(GARSOHn) _____

○ What is the English for ADDITION?
(ADEESEE OHn) _____

○ What is the English for CARTE? (KART) _____

○ What is the English for CUILLER?
(KWEE ER) _____

○ What is the English for FOURCHETTE?
(FOORSHET) _____

○ What is the English for COUTEAU?
(KOOTOH) _____

○ What is the English for RESTAURANT?
(RESTOROn) _____

TURN BACK FOR THE ANSWERS

THINK OF EACH IMAGE IN YOUR MIND'S EYE FOR ABOUT TEN SECONDS

○ The gender of RESTAURANT is MASCULINE   LE RESTAURANT
Imagine a boxer eating in a fashionable restaurant after a fight.

○ The gender of KNIFE is MASCULINE   LE COUTEAU
Imagine a boxer stabbing his opponent with a knife.

○ The gender of FORK is FEMININE   LA FOURCHETTE
Imagine stirring some perfume with a fork.

○ The gender of SPOON is FEMININE   LA CUILLER
Imagine pouring perfume onto a teaspoon and then putting it onto yourself.

○ The gender of MENU is FEMININE   LA CARTE
Imagine a menu that smells of perfume when you sniff it.

○ The gender of BILL is FEMININE   L'ADDITION
Imagine being presented with a bottle of perfume when your bill comes.

○ The gender of WAITER is MASCULINE   LE GARÇON
Imagine a waiter serving you with boxing gloves on.

○ The gender of WAITRESS is FEMININE   LA SERVEUSE
Imagine a waitress smelling of cheap perfume.

○ The gender of CUP is FEMININE   LA TASSE
Imagine a cup full of perfume.

○ The gender of PLATE is FEMININE   L'ASSIETTE
Imagine pouring some perfume onto a plate.

YOU CAN WRITE YOUR ANSWERS IN

○ What is the gender and French for plate?   _____

○ What is the gender and French for cup?   _____

○ What is the gender and French for waitress? _____

○ What is the gender and French for waiter?   _____

○ What is the gender and French for bill?   _____

○ What is the gender and French for menu?   _____

○ What is the gender and French for spoon?   _____

○ What is the gender and French for fork?   _____

○ What is the gender and French for knife?   _____

○ What is the gender and French for
   restaurant?   _____

TURN BACK FOR THE ANSWERS

ELEMENTARY GRAMMAR

When you want to say THE DOGS EAT or THE CATS EAT, etc.,
then the word for EAT is MANGENT.

However, it sounds exactly as before (MOnJ).

This is also true of the word SEE.

So,

  THE DOGS SEE is LES CHIENS VOIENT (pronounced
VWA)

The word HAVE in THE DOGS HAVE is ONT (pronounced OHn)

The word WANT in THE DOGS WANT is VEULENT (pronounced
VeL)

So,

THE DOG WANTS	is	LE CHIEN VEUT
THE DOGS AND THE CATS WANT	is	LES CHIENS ET LES CHATS VEULENT (VeL)

So,

THE DOGS WANT	is	LES CHIENS VEULENT (VeL)
THE DOGS SEE	is	LES CHIENS VOIENT (VWA)
THE DOGS EAT	is	LES CHIENS MANGENT (MOnJ)
THE DOGS HAVE	is	LES CHIENS ONT (OHn)

Now cover up the answers below and translate the following:

(You can write your answers in)

1. THE HEAVY FORKS AND THE GOLD(EN) KNIVES ARE DIRTY
2. THE WAITERS WANT THE LITTLE CUP
3. THE WAITRESSES EAT THE GREEN GRASS
4. THE BOYS HAVE THE BLUE PLATES
5. THE MICE AND THE GEESE SEE THE BIG RESTAURANT

The answers are:

1. LES FOURCHETTES LOURDES ET LES COUTEAUX DORES SONT SALES
2. LES GARÇONS VEULENT LA PETITE TASSE
3. LES SERVEUSES MANGENT L'HERBE VERTE
4. LES GARÇONS ONT LES ASSIETTES BLEUES
5. LES SOURIS ET LES OIES VOIENT LE GRAND RESTAURANT

Now cover up the answers below and translate the following:

(You can write your answers in)

1. LE GARÇON DORE ET LA SERVEUSE SALE MANGENT CINQ POULES
2. LES ASSIETTES JAUNES ONT UNE TASSE ROUGE
3. LE PERE ET LA MERE VEULENT L'ADDITION
4. LES CUILLERS VOIENT LES RESTAURANTS VERTS
5. IL MANGE LA CARTE MAIS LES LAPINS MANGENT LES FOURCHETTES, ET LES TASSESET LES ASSIETTES

The answers are:

1. THE GOLD(EN) WAITER AND THE DIRTY WAITRESS EAT FIVE HENS
2. THE YELLOW PLATES HAVE A RED CUP
3. THE FATHER AND THE MOTHER WANT THE BILL
4. THE SPOONS SEE THE GREEN RESTAURANTS
5. HE EATS THE MENU BUT THE RABBITS EAT THE FORKS, AND THE CUPS AND THE PLATES

SOME MORE RESTAURANT WORDS

THINK OF EACH IMAGE IN YOUR MIND'S EYE FOR ABOUT TEN SECONDS

○ The French for CUTLERY is COUVERT   (KOOVER)
Imagine that you COVER up the cutlery.

○ The French for TABLECLOTH is NAPPE   (NAP)
Imagine taking a NAP on a tablecloth.

○ The French for GLASS is VERRE   (VER)
Imagine telling the waiter that it is not
FAIR that you don't have a glass.

○ The French for DRINK is BOISSON   (BWASOHn)
Imagine asking if you can talk to the
BOSS ON the quiet about whether you can
have free drinks.

○ The French for FOOD is NOURRITURE   (NOOREETooR)
Imagine asking the waiter if there is food to
NOURISH YOUR body.

○ The French for LUNCH is DEJEUNER   (DAYJeNAY)
Imagine asking yourself if this is one of the
DAYS YOU MAY eat lunch.

○ The French for DINNER is DINER   (DEENAY)
Imagine having DINNER in the Eiffel Tower.

○ The French for MEAT is VIANDE   (VEE OnD)
Imagine a German waiter saying "VE
HAND the meat to you."

○ The French for VEGETABLE is LEGUME   (LAYGooM)
Imagine you take gum out of your mouth
when the vegetables are served, and LAY
GUM all round the vegetables.

○ The French for TIP is POURBOIRE   (POORBWAR)
Imagine thinking "This is a POOR BAR. I
won't leave a tip."

YOU CAN WRITE YOUR ANSWERS IN

○ What is the English for POURBOIRE?
(POORBWAR) _____

○ What is the English for LEGUME?
(LAYGoom) _____

○ What is the English for VIANDE?
(VEE OnD) _____

○ What is the English for DINER?
(DEENAY) _____

○ What is the English for DEJEUNER?
(DAYJeNAY) _____

○ What is the English for NOURRITURE?
(NOOREETooR) _____

○ What is the English for BOISSON?
(BWASOHn) _____

○ What is the English for VERRE? (VER) _____

○ What is the English for NAPPE? (NAP) _____

○ What is the English for COUVERT?
(KOOVER) _____

TURN BACK FOR THE ANSWERS

THINK OF EACH IMAGE IN YOUR MIND'S EYE FOR ABOUT TEN SECONDS

○ The gender of CUTLERY is MASCULINE   LE COUVERT
Imagine a boxer laying a table with cutlery.

○ The gender of TABLECLOTH is FEMININE   LA NAPPE
Imagine spraying perfume on a
tablecloth to make it smell nice.

○ The gender of GLASS is MASCULINE   LE VERRE
Imagine a boxer drinking from a glass
before he goes out to fight.

○ The gender of DRINK is FEMININE   LA BOISSON
Imagine your drinks smell strongly of perfume.

○ The gender of FOOD is FEMININE   LA NOURRITURE
Imagine someone spraying all your food
with perfume before a meal.

○ The gender of LUNCH is MASCULINE   LE DEJEUNER
Imagine a boxer tucking into a light
lunch before a fight.

○ The gender of DINNER is MASCULINE   LE DINER
Imagine a boxer celebrating a victory
with a big dinner in an expensive restaurant.

○ The gender of MEAT is FEMININE   LA VIANDE
Imagine marinading meat in perfume.

○ The gender of VEGETABLE is
MASCULINE   LE LEGUME
Imagine a boxer eating a big plate of
vegetables.

○ The gender of TIP is MASCULINE   LE POURBOIRE
Imagine a famous boxer leaving a
miserly tip.

YOU CAN WRITE YOUR ANSWERS IN

○ What is the gender and French for tip?   _____

○ What is the gender and French for vegetable?   _____

○ What is the gender and French for meat?   _____

○ What is the gender and French for dinner?   _____

○ What is the gender and French for lunch?   _____

○ What is the gender and French for food?   _____

○ What is the gender and French for drinks?   _____

○ What is the gender and French for glass?   _____

○ What is the gender and French for tablecloth?   _____

○ What is the gender and French for cutlery?   _____

TURN BACK FOR THE ANSWERS

ELEMENTARY GRAMMAR

When you ask questions in French, you can always do so by keeping the same word order as normal, but putting the words EST-CE QUE first.

(EST-CE QUE is pronounced ESKe)

Imagine you ASK A question.

So,

THE DOGS ARE BLACK	is	LES CHIENS SONT NOIRS
ARE THE DOGS BLACK?	is	EST-CE QUE LES CHIENS SONT NOIRS?
THE RESTAURANT IS DIRTY	is	LE RESTAURANT EST SALE
IS THE RESTAURANT DIRTY?	is	EST-CE QUE LE RESTAURANT EST SALE?

However, if the word which follows EST-CE QUE begins with a vowel then the "E" of QUE is dropped.

For example,

HE IS UGLY is IL EST LAID

IS HE UGLY? is EST-CE QU'IL EST LAID?

Now cover up the answers below and translate the following:

(You can write your answers in)

1. DOES HE EAT THE TIRED FISH OR THE FOOD?
2. DOES SHE HAVE THE DRINKS?
3. DO THE THIN DOGS AND THE BIG CATS EAT THE TABLECLOTH, OR THE MENU?
4. DO THE SEVEN FLIES WANT A YELLOW GLASS?
5. DOES THE LITTLE WAITER WANT A BIG TIP?

The answers are:

1. EST-CE QU'IL MANGE LE POISSON FATIGUE OU LA NOURRITURE?
2. EST-CE QU'ELLE A LES BOISSONS?
3. EST-CE QUE LES CHIENS MINCES ET LES GRANDS CHATS MANGENT LA NAPPE, OU LA CARTE?
4. EST-CE QUE LES SEPT MOUCHES VEULENT UN VERRE JAUNE?
5. EST-CE QUE LE PETIT GARÇON VEUT UN GRAND POURBOIRE?

Now cover up the answers below and translate the following:

(You can write your answers in)

1. EST-CE QUE LA VIANDE EST CHAUDE?
2. EST-CE QU'IL A LE COUVERT?
3. EST-CE QUE LES TROIS GARÇONS VOIENT LES TABLES ROUGES?
4. EST-CE QUE LES POURBOIRES SONT GRANDS?
5. EST-CE QUE LES LEGUMES ET LES VERRES SONT VERTS?

The answers are:

1. IS THE MEAT HOT?
2. HAS HE THE CUTLERY?
3. DO THE THREE BOYS SEE THE RED TABLES?
4. ARE THE TIPS BIG?
5. ARE THE VEGETABLES AND THE GLASSES GREEN?

TELLING THE TIME (1)

THINK OF EACH IMAGE IN YOUR MIND'S EYE FOR ABOUT TEN SECONDS

In order to tell the time in French, you will need to learn a few more words.

○ The French for TEN is DIX   (DEES)
Imagine you DISmiss TEN soldiers.

○ The French for ELEVEN is ONZE·   (OHnZ)
Imagine ON THE stroke of ELEVEN, you
shoot eleven footballers.

○ The French for 12 o'clock (midday) is MIDI
Imagine meeting someone at MIDDAY at   (MEEDEE)
the Eiffel Tower.

○ The French for 12 o'clock (midnight) is
MINUIT   (MEENWEE)
Imagine asking someone "Do you MEAN WE
should see you at MIDNIGHT?"

○ The French for QUARTER is QUART   (KAR)
Imagine you cut a CAR in QUARTERS.

○ The French for HALF is DEMIE   (DeMEE)
Imagine you saw a DUMMY in HALF.

○ The French for TWENTY is VINGT   (VAHn)
Imagine a TWENTY year old VAN.

○ The French for TWENTY-FIVE is
VINGT-CINQ   (VAHnT-SAHnK)
Imagine your VAN SANK into the river at
TWENTY-FIVE past the hour.

YOU CAN WRITE YOUR ANSWERS IN

○ What is the English for VINGT-CINQ?
(VAHnT-SAHnK)   _____

○ What is the English for VINGT? (VAHn)   _____

○ What is the English for DEMIE? (DeMEE)   _____

○ What is the English for QUART? (KAR)   _____

○ What is the English for MINUIT?
(MEENWEE)   _____

○ What is the English for MIDI? (MEEDEE)   _____

○ What is the English for ONZE? (OHnZ)   _____

○ What is the English for DIX? (DEES)   _____

TURN BACK FOR THE ANSWERS

YOU CAN WRITE YOUR ANSWERS IN

○ What is the French for twenty-five? _____

○ What is the French for twenty? _____

○ What is the French for half? _____

○ What is the French for quarter? _____

○ What is the French for 12 o'clock midnight? _____

○ What is the French for 12 o'clock midday? _____

○ What is the French for eleven? _____

○ What is the French for ten? _____

TURN BACK FOR THE ANSWERS

ELEMENTARY GRAMMAR: TELLING THE TIME (2)

As you learned earlier, the French for HOUR is HEURE, which is feminine.

The French for WHAT? is QUELLE (pronounced KEL in the feminine.)

Imagine thinking "WHAT? KILL HER!"

To say WHAT TIME IS IT? you simply say WHAT HOUR IS IT?:

QUELLE HEURE EST-IL? (pronounced KEL eR ET EEL)

To answer the question in French, for example IT IS ONE O'CLOCK, IT IS TWO O'CLOCK, etc., the literal translation is IT IS ONE HOUR, IT IS TWO HOURS, and so on.

So,

IT IS ONE O'CLOCK is IT IS ONE HOUR   (IL EST UNE
                                          HEURE)

IT IS TWO O'CLOCK is IT IS TWO HOURS (IL EST
                                        DEUX
                                        HEURES)

To say IT IS TWELVE O'CLOCK (midday) you say IL EST MIDI

IT IS TWELVE O'CLOCK (midnight) is IL EST MINUIT

and so on.

Now cover up the answers below and translate the following:

(You can write your answers in)

1. IT IS FIVE O'CLOCK
2. IT IS SIX O'CLOCK
3. IT IS 12 O'CLOCK (MIDNIGHT)
4. IT IS TEN O'CLOCK
5. IT IS SEVEN O'CLOCK

The answers are:

1. IL EST CINQ HEURES
2. IL EST SIX HEURES
3. IL EST MINUIT
4. IL EST DIX HEURES
5. IL EST SEPT HEURES

TELLING THE TIME (3)

When you want to say IT IS FIVE PAST SEVEN or TEN PAST EIGHT or TWENTY PAST NINE or TWENTY-FIVE PAST TEN, etc., then you simply put the number of minutes after the hour.

For example,

SEVEN HOURS FIVE (SEPT HEURES CINQ) is FIVE PAST SEVEN

TEN HOURS TEN (DIX HEURES DIX) is TEN PAST TEN

So, to say IT IS FIVE PAST ELEVEN, you just say IL EST ONZE HEURES CINQ.

To say IT IS QUARTER PAST or HALF PAST THE HOUR you simply say, for example, SEVEN HOURS AND QUARTER or SEVEN HOURS AND HALF.

So,

HALF PAST FIVE is CINQ HEURES ET DEMIE

QUARTER PAST THREE is TROIS HEURES ET QUART

Now cover up the answers below and translate the following:

(You can write your answers in)

1. IT IS QUARTER PAST FIVE
2. IT IS TWENTY-FIVE PAST THREE
3. IT IS FIVE PAST ONE
4. IT IS TEN PAST NINE
5. IT IS TWENTY PAST EIGHT

The answers are:

1. IL EST CINQ HEURES ET QUART
2. IIL EST TROIS HEURES VINGT-CINQ
3. IL EST UNE HEURE CINQ
4. IL EST NEUF HEURES DIX
5. IL EST HUIT HEURES VINGT

TELLING THE TIME (4)

If you want to say IT IS FIVE TO SIX, and so on, then in French you say:

   IT IS SIX HOURS MINUS FIVE.

The French for MINUS (or LESS) is MOINS (pronounced MWAHn).

   Imagine you MOAN for LESS.

So,

   IT IS FIVE TO SEVEN is IT IS SEVEN HOURS MINUS FIVE

   (IL EST SEPT HEURES MOINS CINQ)

   IT IS TWENTY TO NINE is IT IS NINE HOURS MINUS TWENTY

   (IL EST NEUF HEURES MOINS VINGT)

There is one final point:

When you want to say IT IS QUARTER TO TEN or QUARTER TO ELEVEN, etc., the "quarter" is LE QUART.

So,

   IT IS QUARTER TO FOUR is IL EST QUATRE HEURES MOINS LE QUART

Now cover up the answers below and translate the following:

(You can write your answers in)

1. IT IS QUARTER TO SIX
2. IT IS HALF PAST FOUR
3. IT IS TWENTY TO MIDNIGHT
4. IT IS TWENTY-FIVE PAST FOUR
5. IT IS FIVE TO ONE
6. IL EST CINQ HEURES MOINS LE QUART
7. IL EST SEPT HEURES ET DEMIE
8. IL EST TROIS HEURES VINGT
9. IL EST MINUIT
10. IL EST ONZE HEURES MOINS DIX

The answers are:

1. IL EST SIX HEURES MOINS LE QUART
2. IL EST QUATRE HEURES ET DEMIE
3. IL EST MINUIT MOINS VINGT
4. IL EST QUATRE HEURES VINGT-CINQ
5. IL EST UNE HEURE MOINS CINQ
6. IT IS QUARTER TO FIVE
7. IT IS HALF PAST SEVEN
8. IT IS TWENTY PAST THREE
9. IT IS MIDNIGHT
10. IT IS TEN TO ELEVEN

Section 6   FOOD AND DRINK

THINK OF EACH IMAGE IN YOUR MIND'S EYE FOR ABOUT TEN SECONDS

○ The French for CABBAGE is CHOU   (SHOO)
Imagine a cabbage growing out of a SHOE.

○ The French for LETTUCE is SALADE   (SALAD)
Imagine a lettuce SALAD.

○ The French for BEAN is HARICOT   (AREEKOH)
Imagine eating HARICOT beans.

○ The French for POTATO is POMME DE   (POM De TER)
TERRE
Imagine Australians throwing potatoes at
Englishmen ("Poms") trying to land in
Australia — the potatoes are POM DETERRents.

○ The French for TOMATO is TOMATE   (TOMAT)
Imagine throwing TOMATOES at the Eiffel Tower.

○ The French for EGG is OEUF   (eF)
Imagine telling a chicken to get OFF her egg.

○ The French for BUTTER is BEURRE   (BeR)
Imagine you hear a cat PURR after it has
eaten some butter.

○ The French for BREAD is PAIN   (PAHn)
Imagine putting loaves of bread in a PAN.

○ The French for MILK is LAIT   (LAY)
Imagine a hen which LAYS a bottle of milk.

○ The French for WATER is EAU   (OH)
Imagine that you OWE a mean Frenchman
for a glass of water.

YOU CAN WRITE YOUR ANSWERS IN

○ What is the English for EAU? (OH) _____

○ What is the English for LAIT? (LAY) _____

○ What is the English for PAIN? (PAHn) _____

○ What is the English for BEURRE? (BeR) _____

○ What is the English for OEUF? (eF) _____

○ What is the English for TOMATE?
(TOMAT) _____

○ What is the English for POMME DE
TERRE? (POM De TER) _____

○ What is the English for HARICOT?
(AREEKOH) _____

○ What is the English for SALADE?
(SALAD) _____

○ What is the English for CHOU? (SHOO) _____

TURN BACK FOR THE ANSWERS

114

THINK OF EACH IMAGE IN YOUR MIND'S EYE FOR ABOUT TEN SECONDS

○ The gender of CABBAGE is MASCULINE   LE CHOU
Imagine a boxer eating a cabbage.

○ The gender of LETTUCE is FEMININE   LA SALADE
Imagine using perfume as a lettuce
dressing — it tastes awful!

○ The gender of BEAN is MASCULINE   LE HARICOT
Imagine a boxer eating baked beans.

○ The gender of POTATO is   LA POMME DE TERRE
FEMININE
Imagine covering your potatoes
with a perfume instead of salt.

○ The gender of TOMATO is FEMININE   LA TOMATE
Imagine crushing tomatoes to make
tomato perfume.

○ The gender of EGG is MASCULINE   L'OEUF
Imagine a boxer filling himself with
raw eggs to make himself stronger.

○ The gender of BUTTER is MASCULINE   LE BEURRE
Imagine a boxer smearing himself
with butter to make himself more
difficult to hit.

○ The gender of BREAD is MASCULINE   LE PAIN
Imagine a boxer stuffing himself
with bread to make himself heavier.

○ The gender of MILK is MASCULINE   LE LAIT
Imagine a boxer drinking pints of
milk to make himself stronger.

○ The gender of WATER is FEMININE   L'EAU
Imagine the perfume "Eau-de-Cologne".

YOU CAN WRITE YOUR ANSWERS IN

○ What is the gender and French for water? _____

○ What is the gender and French for milk? _____

○ What is the gender and French for bread? _____

○ What is the gender and French for butter? _____

○ What is the gender and French for egg? _____

○ What is the gender and French for tomato? _____

○ What is the gender and French for potato? _____

○ What is the gender and French for bean? _____

○ What is the gender and French for lettuce? _____

○ What is the gender and French for cabbage? _____

TURN BACK FOR THE ANSWERS

ELEMENTARY GRAMMAR

The French word for YES is OUI (WEE)

Imagine thinking "YES WE want it."

The French word for NO is NON (NOHn)

Imagine thinking "NO! NO!"

When you want to say NOT in French, for example, SHE DOES NOT EAT then you must say SHE EATS NOT.

The word for NOT is PAS (PA)

Imagine thinking "NOT my PA again drunk."

However, you must also add the word NE (pronounced Ne).

So,

SHE EATS NOT (SHE DOES NOT EAT) is ELLE NE MANGE PAS

For example,

HE DOES NOT WANT THE CABBAGE is HE WANTS NOT THE CABBAGE

(IL NE VEUT PAS LE CHOU)

THE DOG DOES NOT EAT THE CAT is THE DOG EATS NOT THE CAT

(LE CHIEN NE MANGE PAS LE CHAT)

There is one final point:

If the NE comes before a word which starts with a vowel (for example, EST) then NE becomes N'.

So,

IL NE MANGE PAS is HE DOES NOT EAT

but

HE IS NOT BIG is IL N'EST PAS GRAND

Now cover up the answers below and translate the following:

(You can write your answers in)

1. THE GREEN CABBAGE IS NOT DIRTY
2. THE BIG POTATOES ARE NOT BLACK
3. THE QUIET TOMATO DOES NOT SEE THE BLUE BEANS
4. THE GREY EGG AND THE ORANGE BUTTER DO NOT WANT THE GREEN BREAD
5. THE COLD MILK AND THE HOT WATER ARE NOT HEAVY

The answers are:

1. LE CHOU VERT N'EST PAS SALE
2. LES GRANDES POMMES DE TERRE NE SONT PAS NOIRES
3. LA TOMATE TRANQUILLE NE VOIT PAS LES HARICOTS BLEUS
4. L'OEUF GRIS ET LE BEURRE ORANGE NE VEULENT PAS LE PAIN VERT
5. LE LAIT FROID ET L'EAU CHAUDE NE SONT PAS LOURDS

Now cover up the answers below and translate the following:

(You can write your answers in)

1. OUI, IL N'EST PAS ROUGE
2. NON, ELLE NE MANGE PAS LE HERISSON
3. NON, IL NE VOIT PAS LE CHOU
4. LES TOMATES ET LES POMMES DE TERRE NE SONT PAS SALES
5. LE FRERE N'A PAS LES PETITS HARICOTS

The answers are:

1. YES, HE IS NOT RED
2. NO, SHE DOES NOT EAT THE HEDGEHOG
3. NO, HE DOES NOT SEE THE CABBAGE
4. THE TOMATOES AND THE POTATOES ARE NOT DIRTY
5. THE BROTHER DOES NOT HAVE THE LITTLE BEANS

MORE FOOD AND DRINK WORDS

THINK OF EACH IMAGE IN YOUR MIND'S EYE FOR ABOUT TEN SECONDS

○ The French for BEER is BIERE   (BEE ER)
Imagine pouring BEER from the top of
the Eiffel Tower.

○ The French for WINE is VIN   (VAHn)
Imagine a VAN delivering bottles of wine.

○ The French for APPLE is POMME   (POM)
Imagine someone who has an apple on
his head instead of a POM-POM.

○ The French for PEAR is POIRE   (PWAR)
Imagine being so POOR you can only
afford cheap pears.

○ The French for PEACH is PECHE   (PESH)
Imagine a child being a PEST until you
give him a peach.

○ The French for COFFEE is CAFE   (KAFAY)
Imagine drinking coffee in a French CAFE.

○ The French for CHEESE is FROMAGE   (FROMAJ)
Imagine someone who can't tell cheese
FROM MARGarine.

○ The French for MUSHROOM is   (SHOnPEENYOHn)
CHAMPIGNON
Imagine you have raised a CHAMPION
mushroom.

○ The French for GARLIC is AIL   (A EE)
Imagine someone poking you in the
EYE with a piece of garlic.

○ The French for SNAIL is ESCARGOT   (ESKARGOH)
Imagine a ship with ITS CARGO of snails.

YOU CAN WRITE YOUR ANSWERS IN

○ What is the English for ESCARGOT?
(ESKARGOH)   _____

○ What is the English for AIL? (A EE)   _____

○ What is the English for CHAMPIGNON?
(SHOnPEENYOHn)   _____

○ What is the English for FROMAGE?
(FROMAJ)   _____

○ What is the English for CAFE? (KAFAY)   _____

○ What is the English for PECHE? (PESH)   _____

○ What is the English for POIRE? (PWAR)   _____

○ What is the English for POMME? (POM)   _____

○ What is the English for VIN? (VAHn)   _____

○ What is the English for BIERE? (BEE ER)   _____

TURN BACK FOR THE ANSWERS

THINK OF EACH IMAGE IN YOUR MIND'S EYE FOR ABOUT TEN SECONDS

○ The gender of BEER is FEMININE   LA BIERE
Imagine your beer tasting like
perfume — you spit it out.

○ The gender of WINE is MASCULINE   LE VIN
Imagine a boxer drinking a whole bottle
of wine before a fight.

○ The gender of APPLE is FEMININE   LA POMME
Imagine marinading apples in a perfume sauce.

○ The gender of PEAR is FEMININE   LA POIRE
Imagine a perfume that smells of pears.

○ The gender of PEACH is FEMININE   LA PECHE
Imagine using peach brandy as perfume.

○ The gender of COFFEE is MASCULINE   LE CAFE
Imagine boxers drinking coffee after a fight.

○ The gender of CHEESE is MASCULINE   LE FROMAGE
Imagine a boxer filling his gloves with
cheese to make the boxing gloves heavier.

○ The gender of MUSHROOM is   LE CHAMPIGNON
MASCULINE
Imagine a boxer eating a magic
mushroom to make him box better.

○ The gender of GARLIC is MASCULINE   L'AIL
Imagine a boxer breathing garlic at his
opponent to put him off his boxing.

○ The gender of SNAIL is MASCULINE   L'ESCARGOT
Imagine a snail crawling up a boxer's leg
during a fight.

YOU CAN WRITE YOUR ANSWERS IN

○ What is the gender and French for snail? _____

○ What is the gender and French for garlic? _____

○ What is the gender and French for mushroom? _____

○ What is the gender and French for cheese? _____

○ What is the gender and French for coffee? _____

○ What is the gender and French for peach? _____

○ What is the gender and French for pear? _____

○ What is the gender and French for apple? _____

○ What is the gender and French for wine? _____

○ What is the gender and French for beer? _____

TURN BACK FOR THE ANSWERS

SOME MORE USEFUL WORDS

THINK OF EACH IMAGE IN YOUR MIND'S EYE FOR ABOUT TEN SECONDS

○ The French for VERY is TRES   (TRAY)
Imagine a TRAY VERY full.

○ The French for SOON is BIENTOT   (BEE AHnTOH)
Imagine thinking "I will have BEEN TO
that place SOON."

○ The French for HERE is ICI   (EESEE)
Imagine thinking "It is very EASY HERE
to learn French."

○ The French for THERE is LA   (LA)
Imagine thinking "I might get some ooh
LA LA there!"

○ The French for QUITE is ASSEZ   (ASAY)
Imagine thinking "I SAY, he is QUITE clever."

○ The French for EASY is FACILE   (FASEEL)
Imagine thinking "He has an EASY but
FACILE manner."

○ The French for DIFFICULT is   (DEEFEESEEL)
DIFFICILE
Imagine it is DIFFICULT to climb the
Eiffel Tower.

○ The French for HIGH is HAUT   (OH)
Imagine thinking "OH, I am very HIGH up."

○ The French for ANGRY is FACHE   (FASHAY)
Imagine a very ANGRY FASCIST.

○ The French for GOOD is BON   (BOHn)
Imagine eating GOOD BON bons — bon
bons are goody goodies.

YOU CAN WRITE YOUR ANSWERS IN

○ What is the English for BON? (BOHn) _____

○ What is the English for FACHE?
(FASHAY) _____

○ What is the English for HAUT? (OH) _____

○ What is the English for DIFFICILE?
(DEEFEESEEL) _____

○ What is the English for FACILE?
(FASEEL) _____

○ What is the English for ASSEZ? (ASAY) _____

○ What is the English for LA? (LA) _____

○ What is the English for ICI? (EESEE) _____

○ What is the English for BIENTOT?
(BEE AHnTOH) _____

○ What is the English for TRES? (TRAY) _____

TURN BACK FOR THE ANSWERS

YOU CAN WRITE YOUR ANSWERS IN

○ What is the French for very?   _____

○ What is the French for soon?   _____

○ What is the French for here?   _____

○ What is the French for there?   _____

○ What is the French for quite?   _____

○ What is the French for easy?   _____

○ What is the French for difficult?   _____

○ What is the French for high?   _____

○ What is the French for angry?   _____

○ What is the French for good?   _____

TURN BACK FOR THE ANSWERS

ELEMENTARY GRAMMAR: WAS AND WERE

The French for the words WAS and WERE are pronounced AYTAY, although they are spelt differently.

ETAIT   is WAS.

ETAIENT is WERE.

Imagine wishing I WAS EIGHTY again.

So,

THE DOG WAS BLUE   is LE CHIEN ETAIT BLEU

THE DOGS WERE BLUE   is LES CHIENS ETAIENT
                                              BLEUS

I WAS is J'ETAIS (pronounced JAYTAY)

Now cover up the answers below and translate the following:

(You can write your answers in)

1. THE COLD BEER WAS VERY GOOD

2. THE APPLES AND THE PEARS WERE NOT VERY RED

3. THE BLACK COFFEE AND THE WHITE CHEESE SEE A VERY BIG RESTAURANT

4. THE SNAILS DO NOT EAT A THIN MUSHROOM

5. THE LUNCH AND THE DINNER WERE QUITE GOOD, BUT THE VEGETABLES ARE NOT VERY HOT

The answers are:

1. LA BIERE FROIDE ETAIT TRES BONNE

2. LES POMMES ET LES POIRES N'ETAIENT PAS TRES ROUGES

3. LE CAFE NOIR ET LE FROMAGE BLANC VOIENT UN TRES GRAND RESTAURANT

4. LES ESCARGOTS NE MANGENT PAS UN CHAMPIGNON MINCE

5. LE DEJEUNER ET LE DINER ETAIENT ASSEZ BONS, MAIS LES LEGUMES NE SONT PAS TRES CHAUDS

Now cover up the answers below and translate the following:

(You can write your answers in)

1. LE VIN N'ETAIT PAS ICI
2. LES PECHES ET L'AIL ETAIENT TRES BONS
3. LE MARI ETAIT ASSEZ FACHE, MAIS LA FEMME ETAIT TRES TRANQUILLE
4. LES GARÇONS ETAIENT TRES DIFFICILES, MAIS LES SERVEUSES ETAIENT TRES BONNES
5. LE PLAFOND ETAIT TRES HAUT

The answers are:

1. THE WINE WAS NOT HERE
2. THE PEACHES AND THE GARLIC WERE VERY GOOD
3. THE HUSBAND WAS QUITE ANGRY, BUT THE WIFE WAS VERY QUIET
4. THE WAITERS WERE VERY DIFFICULT, BUT THE WAITRESSES WERE VERY GOOD
5. THE CEILING WAS VERY HIGH

Section 7   SHOPPING AND BUSINESS WORDS

THINK OF EACH IMAGE IN YOUR MIND'S EYE FOR ABOUT TEN SECONDS

○ The French for WORKER is OUVRIER   (OOVREE AY)
  Imagine a worker shouting at you "I'm
  OVER HERE."

○ The French for COMPANY (FIRM) is   (KOHnPANYEE)
  COMPAGNIE
  Imagine your COMPANY buying the Eiffel Tower.

○ The French for FACTORY is USINE   (ooZEEN)
  Imagine asking "Have YOU SEEN the factory?"

○ The French for MANAGER is DIRECTEUR   (DEEREKTeR)
  Imagine that when you ask to see the
  manager, you are shown into the Managing
  DIRECTOR's office.

○ The French for BOSS is PATRON   (PATROHn)
  Imagine the boss of a business being very
  PATRONising to you.

○ The French for OFFICE is BUREAU   (BooROH)
  Imagine a writing BUREAU in an office.

○ The French for SHOP is MAGASIN   (MAGAZAHn)
  Imagine every shop you go into sells MAGAZINES.

○ The French for PRICE is PRIX   (PREE)
  Imagine asking the price of admission to
  see a Grand PRIX race.
  (N.B. PRIX also means prize).

○ The French for CHEQUE is CHEQUE   (SHEK)
  Imagine paying by CHEQUE to get into
  the Eiffel Tower.

○ The French for SALARY is SALAIRE   (SALER)
  Imagine being paid your SALARY at the
  top of the Eiffel Tower.

YOU CAN WRITE YOUR ANSWERS IN

○ What is the English for SALAIRE?
(SALER)   _____

○ What is the English for CHEQUE? (SHEK) _____

○ What is the English for PRIX? (PREE)   _____

○ What is the English for MAGASIN?
(MAGAZAHn)   _____

○ What is the English for BUREAU?
(BooROH)   _____

○ What is the English for PATRON?
(PATROHn)   _____

○ What is the English for DIRECTEUR?
(DEEREKTeR)   _____

○ What is the English for USINE? (ooZEEN) _____

○ What is the English for COMPAGNIE?
(KOHnPANYEE)   _____

○ What is the English for OUVRIER?
(OOVREE AY)   _____

TURN BACK FOR THE ANSWERS

132

THINK OF EACH IMAGE IN YOUR MIND'S EYE FOR ABOUT TEN SECONDS

○ The gender of WORKER is MASCULINE   L'OUVRIER
Imagine a worker stripping off for a boxing match.

○ The gender of COMPANY (FIRM) is   LA COMPAGNIE
FEMININE
Imagine a company which makes perfumes.

○ The gender of FACTORY is FEMININE   L'USINE
Imagine a factory making perfume.

○ The gender of MANAGER is   LE DIRECTEUR
MASCULINE
Imagine a boxing manager.

○ The gender of BOSS is MASCULINE   LE PATRON
Imagine the boss of a boxing school,
smoking a fat cigar.

○ The gender of OFFICE is MASCULINE   LE BUREAU
Imagine a boxer waiting in his manager's office.

○ The gender of SHOP is MASCULINE   LE MAGASIN
Imagine a boxer going wild in a shop,
scattering all the goods.

○ The gender of PRICE is MASCULINE   LE PRIX
Imagine a boxer asking the price of goods.

○ The gender of CHEQUE is MASCULINE   LE CHEQUE
Imagine a boxer being presented with a
cheque after winning a fight.

○ The gender of SALARY is MASCULINE   LE SALAIRE
Imagine a boxer collecting a salary once
a month, even though he does not fight.

YOU CAN WRITE YOUR ANSWERS IN

○ What is the gender and French for salary? _____

○ What is the gender and French for cheque? _____

○ What is the gender and French for price? _____

○ What is the gender and French for shop? _____

○ What is the gender and French for office? _____

○ What is the gender and French for boss? _____

○ What is the gender and French for manager? _____

○ What is the gender and French for factory? _____

○ What is the gender and French for company (firm)? _____

○ What is the gender and French for worker? _____

TURN BACK FOR THE ANSWERS

SOME MORE USEFUL WORDS

THINK OF EACH IMAGE IN YOUR MIND'S EYE FOR ABOUT TEN SECONDS

○ The French for WHERE is OU   (OO)
Imagine thinking "OOH! WHERE are you?"

○ The French for WHY is POURQUOI   (POORKWA)
Imagine thinking "WHY is that
POOR QUACKING duck ill?"

○ The French for HOW is COMMENT   (COMOn)
Imagine saying "HOW well you have COME ON."

○ The French for WHEN is QUAND   (KOn)
Imagine asking WHEN the CON man called.

○ The French for BECAUSE is PARCE QUE   (PARS Ke)
Imagine saying you PASSED HER the salt
BECAUSE she asked for it.

YOU CAN WRITE YOUR ANSWERS IN

○ What is the English for PARCE QUE?
(PARS Ke) _____

○ What is the English for QUAND? (KOn) _____

○ What is the English for COMMENT?
(KOMOn) _____

○ What is the English for POURQUOI?
(POORKWA) _____

○ What is the English for OU? (OO) _____

TURN BACK FOR THE ANSWERS

YOU CAN WRITE YOUR ANSWERS IN

○ What is the French for because?   _____

○ What is the French for when?   _____

○ What is the French for how?   _____

○ What is the French for why?   _____

○ What is the French for where?   _____

TURN BACK FOR THE ANSWERS

ELEMENTARY GRAMMAR

The words WHERE, WHY, WHEN, HOW are sometimes used with the word EST-CE QUE when asking questions.

As you learned earlier, you use EST-CE QUE when you want to turn a sentence that already exists into a question.

For example,

IS THE WORKER BLUE? is a question, so you should put EST-CE QUE in front:

   EST-CE QUE L'OUVRIER EST BLEU?

WHY IS THE WORKER BLUE? is POURQUOI EST-CE QUE L'OUVRIER EST BLEU?

WHEN IS THE ROOF DIRTY?   is QUAND EST-CE QUE LE TOIT EST SALE?

Here is another example:

   HOW DOES THE BOSS WANT THE FISH?

   is COMMENT EST-CE QUE LE PATRON VEUT LE POISSON?

However, if you just want to say WHERE IS or WHERE ARE, you simply say:

   OU EST or OU SONT

   without the EST-CE QUE.

So,

   WHERE   IS   THE   BOSS? is OU   EST   LE   PATRON?

Now cover up the answers below and translate the following:

(You can write your answers in)

1. WHERE IS THE OFFICE?
2. WHY IS THE SHOP QUIET?
3. HOW DOES HE EAT THE DUCK?
4. WHEN ARE THE FACTORIES QUIET?
5. WHERE IS THE WORKER?

The answers are:

1. OU EST LE BUREAU?
2. POURQUOI EST-CE QUE LE MAGASIN EST TRANQUILLE?
3. COMMENT EST-CE QU'IL MANGE LE CANARD?
4. QUAND EST-CE QUE LES USINES SONT TRANQUILLES?
5. OU EST L'OUVRIER?

Now cover up the answers below and translate the following:

(You can write your answers in)

1. POURQUOI EST-CE QUE LE DIRECTEUR EST FACHE?
2. OU EST LE PATRON ET OU EST LA COMPAGNIE?
3. COMMENT EST-CE QUE L'OUVRIER VOIT LE CHEQUE?
4. QUAND EST-CE QUE LE PATRON MANGE LE SALAIRE?
5. OU SONT LES PRIX ET OU SONT LES CHEQUES?

The answers are:

1. WHY IS THE MANAGER ANGRY?
2. WHERE IS THE BOSS AND WHERE IS THE COMPANY?
3. HOW DOES THE WORKER SEE THE CHEQUE?
4. WHEN DOES THE BOSS EAT THE SALARY?
5. WHERE ARE THE PRICES AND WHERE ARE THE CHEQUES?

MORE SHOPPING AND BUSINESS WORDS

THINK OF EACH IMAGE IN YOUR MIND'S EYE FOR ABOUT TEN SECONDS

○ The French for RECEIPT is REÇU   (ReSoo)
Imagine someone RESCUING a receipt from you.

○ The French for MISTAKE is ERREUR   (EReR)
Imagine being told that ERRORS and
mistakes cannot be rectified.

○ The French for HOLIDAYS is VACANCES   (VAKOnS)
Imagine all the staff have gone on their
holidays during the VACATION.

○ The French for CASH TILL is CAISSE   (KES)
Imagine putting a cash till in a CASE.

○ The French for GOODS is   (MARSHOnDEEZ)
MARCHANDISE
Imagine selling goods and MERCHANDISE.

○ The French for ACCOUNTANT is   (KOHnTABL)
COMPTABLE
Imagine thinking your accountant is CONTEMPTIBLE.

○ The French for CONTRACT is CONTRAT   (KOHnTRA)
Imagine signing a CONTRACT to buy
the Eiffel Tower.

○ The French for STRIKER IS GREVISTE   (GRAYVEEST)
Imagine a GREY VEST on a striker
outside a factory.

○ The French for SALESMAN is VENDEUR   (VOnDeR)
Imagine a salesman trying to sell you a VAN DOOR.

○ The French for SECRETARY is   (SeKRAYTER)
SECRETAIRE
Imagine a pretty SECRETARY jumping
from the Eiffel Tower.

YOU CAN WRITE YOUR ANSWERS IN

○ What is the English for SECRETAIRE?
(SeKRAYTER) _____

○ What is the English for VENDEUR?
(VOnDeR) _____

○ What is the English for GREVISTE?
(GRAYVEEST) _____

○ What is the English for CONTRAT?
(KOHnTRA) _____

○ What is the English for COMPTABLE?
(KOHnTABL) _____

○ What is the English for MARCHANDISE?
(MARSHOnDEEZ) _____

○ What is the English for CAISSE? (KES) _____

○ What is the English for VACANCES?
(VAKOnS) _____

○ What is the English for ERREUR? (EReR) _____

○ What is the English for REÇU? (ReSoo) _____

TURN BACK FOR THE ANSWERS

THINK OF EACH IMAGE IN YOUR MIND'S EYE FOR ABOUT TEN SECONDS

○ The gender of RECEIPT is MASCULINE   LE REÇU
  Imagine a boxer asking for a receipt
  for his prize.

○ The gender of MISTAKE is FEMININE   L'ERREUR
  Imagine putting on perfume by mistake.

○ The gender of HOLIDAYS is   LES VACANCES
  FEMININE
  Imagine bringing some bottles of
  perfume from your holidays.

○ The gender of CASH TILL is FEMININE   LA CAISSE
  Imagine a shop assistant ringing up a
  payment for perfume on a cash till.

○ The gender of GOODS is   LA MARCHANDISE
  FEMININE
  Imagine buying goods which include
  boxes of perfume.

○ The gender of ACCOUNTANT is   LE COMPTABLE
  MASCULINE
  Imagine a boxer talking to his
  accountant about his tax problems.

○ The gender of CONTRACT is MASCULINE   LE CONTRAT
  Imagine boxers going over a contract to fight.

○ The gender of STRIKER is MASCULINE   LE GREVISTE
  Imagine two boxers striking each other.
  (But remember STRIKER has a different meaning.)

○ The gender of SALESMAN is MASCULINE   LE VENDEUR
  Imagine a salesman selling miniature boxers.

○ The gender of SECRETARY is   LA SECRETAIRE
  FEMININE
  Imagine a secretary covering herself
  with perfume.

YOU CAN WRITE YOUR ANSWERS IN

○ What is the gender and French for
secretary?   _____

○ What is the gender and French for
salesman?   _____

○ What is the gender and French for striker?   _____

○ What is the gender and French for contract?   _____

○ What is the gender and French for
accountant?   _____

○ What is the gender and French for goods?   _____

○ What is the gender and French for cash till? _____

○ What is the gender and French for holidays?   _____

○ What is the gender and French for mistake?   _____

○ What is the gender and French for receipt?   _____

TURN BACK FOR THE ANSWERS

ADJECTIVES

THINK OF EACH IMAGE IN YOUR MIND'S EYE FOR ABOUT TEN SECONDS

○ The French for YOUNG is JEUNE (JeN)
Imagine getting drunk on GIN when you are YOUNG.

○ The French for CLEAN is PROPRE (PROPR)
Imagine looking CLEAN and PROPER.

○ The French for HARD is DUR (DooR)
Imagine something HARD and DURABLE.

○ The French for FULL is PLEIN (PLAHn)
Imagine a FULL PLAN of action.

○ The French for DRY is SEC (SEK)
Imagine putting DRY clothes in a SACK.
(N.B. The feminine of SEC is SECHE [SESH])

○ The French for WIDE is LARGE (LARJ)
Imagine a LARGE, WIDE hole.

○ The French for NARROW is ETROIT (AYTRWA)
Imagine IT WERE a NARROW opening.

○ The French for SHORT is COURT (KOOR)
Imagine trying to CURE a SHORT man of his cold.

○ The French for STUPID is STUPIDE (STooPEED)
Imagine someone STUPID jumping from the
Eiffel Tower.

YOU CAN WRITE YOUR ANSWERS IN

○ What is the English for STUPIDE?
  (STooPEED)   _____

○ What is the English for COURT? (KOOR)   _____

○ What is the English for ETROIT?
  (AYTRWA)   _____

○ What is the English for LARGE? (LARJ)   _____

○ What is the English for SEK? (SEK)   _____

○ What is the English for PLEIN? (PLAHn)   _____

○ What is the English for DUR? (DooR)   _____

○ What is the English for PROPRE?
  (PROPR)   _____

○ What is the English for JEUNE? (JeN)   _____

TURN BACK FOR THE ANSWERS

YOU CAN WRITE THE ANSWERS IN

○ What is the French for stupid?   _____

○ What is the French for short?   _____

○ What is the French for narrow?   _____

○ What is the French for wide?   _____

○ What is the French for dry?   _____

○ What is the French for full?   _____

○ What is the French for hard?   _____

○ What is the French for clean?   _____

○ What is the French for young?   _____

TURN BACK FOR THE ANSWERS

ELEMENTARY GRAMMAR

The French for YOU is VOUS (VOO)

Imagine YOU VIEW something.

In French a verb such as EAT, SEE, WANT, etc., nearly always has an ending EZ (pronounced AY) when you use the word YOU.

So,

I EAT   is JE MANGE (MOnJ)

YOU EAT is VOUS MANGEZ (MOnJAY)

I SEE   is JE VOIS (VWA)

YOU SEE is VOUS VOYEZ (VWAYAY)

There are some verbs which change slightly in the middle when used with the word VOUS.

For example,

I WANT   is JE VEUX(Ve)

YOU WANT is VOUS VOULEZ (VOOLAY)

It adds an EZ, but the EUX becomes OUL.

Do not worry about this, however, you will pick it up as we go along.

SOME USEFUL VERBS

THINK OF EACH IMAGE IN YOUR MIND'S EYE FOR ABOUT TEN SECONDS

○ The French for I AM is JE SUIS   (Je SWEE)
Imagine I AM a SWEDE.

○ The French for I SEE is JE VOIS   (Je VWA)
Imagine I SEE FAR.

○ The French for I WANT is JE VEUX   (Je Ve)
Imagine I WANT your FUR for something.

○ The French for I EAT is JE MANGE   (Je MOnJ)
Imagine I EAT blancMANGE.

○ The French for I HAVE is J'AI   (JAY)
Imagine I HAVE been JAY walking.

○ The French for YOU ARE is VOUS ETES   (VOOZ ET)
Imagine someone saying WHO SAID YOU ARE here.

○ The French for YOU SEE is VOUS   (VOO VWA YAY)
VOYEZ
Imagine someone shouting "I'll SEE YOU
on a VOYAGE."

○ The French for YOU WANT is VOUS   (VOO VOOLAY)
VOULEZ
Imagine YOU WANT a WOOLEN jumper.

○ The French for YOU HAVE is VOUS AVEZ   (VOOZ AVAY)
Imagine YOU HAVE given something AWAY.

○ The French for YOU EAT is VOUS MANGEZ   (VOO MOnJay)
Imagine YOU EAT a MANGY cat.

YOU CAN WRITE YOUR ANSWERS IN

○ What is the English for VOUS MANGEZ?
(VOO MOnJAY)   _____

○ What is the English for VOUS AVEZ?
(VOOZ AVAY)   _____

○ What is the English for VOUS VOULEZ?
(VOO VOOLAY)   _____

○ What is the English for VOUS VOYEZ?
(VOO VWA YAY)   _____

○ What is the English for VOUS ETES?
(VOOZ ET)   _____

○ What is the English for J'AI? (JAY)   _____

○ What is the English for JE MANGE?
(Je MOnJ)   _____

○ What is the English for JE VEUX? (Je Ve)   _____

○ What is the English for JE VOIS? (Je
VWA)   _____

○ What is the English for JE SUIS? (Je
SWEE)   _____

TURN BACK FOR THE ANSWERS

150

YOU CAN WRITE YOUR ANSWERS IN

○ What is the French for I am? _____

○ What is the French for I see? _____

○ What is the French for I want? _____

○ What is the French for I eat? _____

○ What is the French for I have? _____

○ What is the French for you are? _____

○ What is the French for you see? _____

○ What is the French for you want? _____

○ What is the French for you have? _____

○ What is the French for you eat? _____

TURN BACK FOR THE ANSWERS

Now cover up the answers below and translate the following:

(You can write your answers in)

1. YOU ARE THE YOUNG ACCOUNTANT, AND I AM THE LITTLE WORKER

2. ARE YOU THE CLEAN SECRETARY? NO, I AM THE DIRTY MANAGER

3. DO YOU WANT A SALESMAN? YES, I WANT A SALESMAN

4. DO YOU EAT THE RABBIT? YES, I EAT THE RABBIT

5. YOU ARE VERY STUPID, BUT THE RECEIPT IS DRY

The answers are:

1. VOUS ETES LE JEUNE COMPTABLE, ET JE SUIS LE PETIT OUVRIER

2. EST-CE QUE VOUS ETES LA SECRETAIRE PROPRE? NON, JE SUIS LE DIRECTEUR SALE

3. EST-CE QUE VOUS VOULEZ UN VENDEUR? OUI, JE VEUX UN VENDEUR

4. EST-CE QUE VOUS MANGEZ LE LAPIN? OUI, JE MANGE LE LAPIN

5. VOUS ETES TRES STUPIDE, MAIS LE REÇU EST SEC

Now cover up the answers below and translate the following:

(You can write your answers in)

1. VOUS NE MANGEZ PAS LE CHOU, MAIS JE MANGE L'HUITRE
2. JE VEUX LA MARCHANDISE, ET VOUS VOULEZ LA SECRETAIRE
3. JE VOIS L'ERREUR STUPIDE ET VOUS VOYEZ LE CONTRAT SALE
4. LES VACANCES SONT DURES
5. POURQUOI EST-CE QUE VOUS ETES TRES STUPIDE?

The answers are:

1. YOU DO NOT EAT THE CABBAGE, BUT I EAT THE OYSTER
2. I WANT THE GOODS AND YOU WANT THE SECRETARY
3. I SEE THE STUPID MISTAKE AND YOU SEE THE DIRTY CONTRACT
4. THE HOLIDAYS ARE HARD
5. WHY ARE YOU VERY STUPID?

Section 8 TRAVELLING, THE CAR

THINK OF EACH IMAGE IN YOUR MIND'S EYE FOR ABOUT TEN SECONDS

○ The French for PASSPORT is PASSEPORT　　　　(PASPOR)
Imagine your PASSPORT has a picture of
the Eiffel Tower on the front.

○ The French for CUSTOMS is DOUANE　　　　　(DWAN)
Imagine going through customs counting
"D'ONE, D'two, D'three."

○ The French for TOILET is TOILETTES　　　　(TWALET)
Imagine a TOILET right at the top of the
Eiffel Tower.

○ The French for ENTRANCE is ENTREE　　　　(OnTRAY)
Imagine making your entrance ON a TRAY.

○ The French for EXIT is SORTIE　　　　　　(SORTEE)
Imagine having SORE TEETH after
bumping them at the exit of a cinema.

○ The French for SUITCASE is VALISE　　　　(VALEEZ)
Imagine suitcases strewn all over the VALLEYS.

○ The French for TICKET is BILLET　　　　　(BEE AY)
Imagine buying a ticket for a BA (British
Airways) flight.

○ The French for MONEY EXCHANGE is CHANGE　(SHOnJ)
Imagine CHANGING your money at the
money exchange.

○ The French for MONEY is ARGENT　　　　　(ARJOn)
Imagine needing money to go to the ARGENTine.
(N.B. ARGENT is also the word for SILVER.)

○ The French for PEDESTRIAN is PIETON　　(PEE AYTOHn)
Imagine that in France you have to PAY TO
be a pedestrian.

YOU CAN WRITE YOUR ANSWERS IN

○ What is the English for PIETON?
(PEE AYTOHn) _____

○ What is the English for ARGENT?
(ARJOn) _____

○ What is the English for CHANGE?
(SHOnJ) _____

○ What is the English for BILLET?
(BEE AY) _____

○ What is the English for VALISE?
(VALEEZ) _____

○ What is the English for SORTIE?
(SORTEE) _____

○ What is the English for ENTREE?
(OnTRAY) _____

○ What is the English for TOILETTES?
(TWALET) _____

○ What is the English for DOUANE?
(DWAN) _____

○ What is the English for PASSEPORT?
(PASPOR) _____

TURN BACK FOR THE ANSWERS

THINK OF EACH IMAGE IN YOUR MIND'S EYE FOR ABOUT TEN SECONDS

○ The gender of PASSPORT is MASCULINE **LE PASSEPORT**
Imagine a boxer showing his passport with his boxing gloves on.

○ The gender of CUSTOMS is FEMININE **LA DOUANE**
Imagine people trying to smuggle perfume through the customs.

○ The gender of TOILET is FEMININE **LES TOILETTES**
Imagine a toilet where the smell is sweetened by perfume.
NB. TOILET (TOILETTES) is usually plural in French.

○ The gender of ENTRANCE IS FEMININE **L'ENTREE**
Imagine the entrance to your hotel smells strongly of perfume.

○ The gender of EXIT is FEMININE **LA SORTIE**
Imagine the exit to your hotel is also sweetened by perfume.

○ The gender of SUITCASE is FEMININE **LA VALISE**
Imagine your suitcase filled with bottles of perfume.

○ The gender of TICKET is MASCULINE **LE BILLET**
Imagine buying a ticket to get into the boxing match.

○ The gender of MONEY EXCHANGE is MASCULINE **LE CHANGE**
Imagine you meet a boxer at the money exchange.

○ The gender of MONEY is MASCULINE **L'ARGENT**
Imagine you pay a boxer in money for his prize.

○ The gender of PEDESTRIAN is MASCULINE **LE PIETON**
Imagine a lot of pedestrian boxers, dressed only in shorts, crossing the road.

YOU CAN WRITE YOUR ANSWERS IN

○ What is the gender and French for
pedestrian? _____

○ What is the gender and French for money? _____

○ What is the gender and French for money
exchange? _____

○ What is the gender and French for ticket? _____

○ What is the gender and French for suitcase? _____

○ What is the gender and French for exit? _____

○ What is the gender and French for
entrance? _____

○ What is the gender and French for toilet? _____

○ What is the gender and French for customs? _____

○ What is the gender and French for
passport? _____

TURN BACK FOR THE ANSWERS

SOME MORE USEFUL WORDS

THINK OF EACH IMAGE IN YOUR MIND'S EYE FOR ABOUT TEN SECONDS

○ The French for ON is SUR   (SooR)
   Imagine sitting ON a SEWER.

○ The French for UNDER is SOUS   (SOO)
   Imagine talking to a girl called SUE UNDER a table.

○ The French for WITH is AVEC   (AVEK)
   Imagine a German saying "I VAKE up every
   morning WITH a headache."

○ The French for IN is DANS   (DOn)
   Imagine you look IN despair as DAWN breaks.

○ The French for TO or AT is A   (A)
   Imagine thinking "AH! TO AND AT are the same."

YOU CAN WRITE YOUR ANSWERS IN

○ What is the English for A? (A) _____

○ What is the English for DANS? (DOn) _____

○ What is the English for AVEC? (AVEK) _____

○ What is the English for SOUS? (SOO) _____

○ What is the English for SUR? (SooR) _____

TURN BACK FOR THE ANSWERS

YOU CAN WRITE YOUR ANSWERS IN

○ What is the French for to or at?   _____

○ What is the French for in?   _____

○ What is the French for with?   _____

○ What is the French for under?   _____

○ What is the French for on?   _____

TURN BACK FOR THE ANSWERS

ELEMENTARY GRAMMAR
To use the words ON, UNDER, etc., is very simple. You usually use them in the same way as in English.

So,

ON THE TABLE is SUR LA TABLE

etc.

Now cover up the answers below and translate the following:

(You can write your answers in)

1. HE IS AT THE ENTRANCE OR AT THE EXIT
2. THE PEDESTRIAN IS WITH THE FATHER, THE
    DAUGHTER AND THE SON
3. THE MONEY IS IN THE SUITCASE
4. THE TOILETS ARE UNDER THE CASH TILL
5. IS THE PASSPORT IN THE TOILET?

The answers are:

1. IL EST A L'ENTRÉE OU A LA SORTIE
2. LE PIETON EST AVEC LE PERE, LA FILLE ET LE FILS
3. L'ARGENT EST DANS LA VALISE
4. LES TOILETTES SONT SOUS LA CAISSE
5. EST-CE QUE LE PASSEPORT EST DANS LES
    TOILETTES?

Now cover up the answers below and translate the following:

(You can write your answers in)

1. LA DOUANE EST DANS LE JARDIN
2. LE PASSEPORT EST SUR LA VALISE ET LE BILLET EST SUR LA TABLE
3. LE CHANGE EST DANS LES TOILETTES
4. L'ARGENT EST AVEC LE BILLET
5. LE PIETON EST A LA DOUANE

The answers are:

1. THE CUSTOMS ARE IN THE GARDEN
2. THE PASSPORT IS ON THE SUITCASE AND THE TICKET IS ON THE TABLE
3. THE MONEY EXCHANGE IS IN THE TOILET(S)
4. THE MONEY IS WITH THE TICKET
5. THE PEDESTRIAN IS AT THE CUSTOMS

SOME MORE TRAVELLING WORDS

THINK OF EACH IMAGE IN YOUR MIND'S EYE FOR ABOUT TEN SECONDS

○ The French for GARAGE is GARAGE (GARAJ)
Imagine a GARAGE under the Eiffel Tower.

○ The French for ROAD is ROUTE (ROOT)
Imagine roads covered in plant ROOTS.

○ The French for BRIDGE is PONT (POHn)
Imagine smelling a terrible PONG as you cross a bridge.

○ The French for CAR is AUTO (OTOH)
Imagine your car has AUTOmatic gears.

○ The French for BOAT is BATEAU (BATOH)
Imagine going into BATTLE on a boat.

○ The French for OIL is HUILE (WEEL)
Imagine your WHEEL splashing through a pool of oil.

○ The French for PETROL is ESSENCE (ESOnS)
Imagine putting vanilla ESSENCE in your petrol.

○ The French for JACK is CRIC (KREEK)
Imagine being up the CREEK without a jack when
you have a puncture.

○ The French for TYRE is PNEU (PNe)
Imagine needing a NEW tyre.

○ The French for SPANNER is CLEF (KLAY)
Imagine having a CLAY spanner which falls to bits
when you try to use it.
(N.B. CLEF also means KEY).

YOU CAN WRITE YOUR ANSWERS IN

○ What is the English for CLEF? (KLAY)   _____

○ What is the English for PNEU? (PNe)   _____

○ What is the English for CRIC? (KREEK)   _____

○ What is the English for ESSENCE?
(ESOnS)   _____

○ What is the English for HUILE? (WEEL)   _____

○ What is the English for BATEAU?
(BATOH)   _____

○ What is the English for AUTO? (OTOH)   _____

○ What is the English for PONT? (POHn)   _____

○ What is the English for ROUTE? (ROOT)   _____

○ What is the English for GARAGE?
(GARAJ)   _____

TURN BACK FOR THE ANSWERS

THINK OF EACH IMAGE IN YOUR MIND'S EYE FOR ABOUT TEN SECONDS

○ The gender of GARAGE is MASCULINE   LE GARAGE
Imagine boxers fighting in your garage.

○ The gender of ROAD is FEMININE   LA ROUTE
Imagine spraying the road with perfume.

○ The gender of BRIDGE is MASCULINE   LE PONT
Imagine boxers fighting on a bridge.

○ The gender of CAR is FEMININE   L'AUTO
Imagine perfuming your car to make it smell nicer.

○ The gender of BOAT is MASCULINE   LE BATEAU
Imagine a boat full of boxers.

○ The gender of OIL is FEMININE   L'HUILE
Imagine your oil smells of perfume.

○ The gender of PETROL is FEMININE   L'ESSENCE
Imagine putting perfume rather than petrol in your car.

○ The gender of JACK is MASCULINE   LE CRIC
Imagine a boxer hitting his opponent with a jack.

○ The gender of TYRE is MASCULINE   LE PNEU
Imagine a boxer with a tyre round his middle.

○ The gender of SPANNER is FEMININE   LA CLEF
Imagine keeping your spanners soaked in a bottle of perfume.

YOU CAN WRITE THE ANSWERS IN

○ What is the gender and French for spanner?   _____

○ What is the gender and French for tyre?   _____

○ What is the gender and French for jack?   _____

○ What is the gender and French for petrol?   _____

○ What is the gender and French for oil?   _____

○ What is the gender and French for boat?   _____

○ What is the gender and French for car?   _____

○ What is the gender and French for bridge?   _____

○ What is the gender and French for road?   _____

○ What is the gender and French for garage?   _____

TURN BACK FOR THE ANSWERS

ELEMENTARY GRAMMAR
You will remember that if you want to say:
HE DOES NOT EAT THE FISH or HE DOES NOT WANT
                                        THE CUSTOMS

you say,

IL NE MANGE PAS LE POISSON or IL NE VEUT PAS LA
                                        DOUANE

However, to say

  HE WANTS THE CAR, NOT THE BOAT

you simply say PAS for NOT:

  IL VEUT L'AUTO, PAS LE BATEAU

Now cover up the answers below and translate the following:

(You can write your answers in)

1. I SEE THE BRIDGE BUT NOT THE NARROW ROAD
2. SHE HAS THE PETROL BUT NOT THE OIL
3. HE DOES NOT SEE THE JACK
4. HE IS NOT YOUNG, BUT I AM NOT CLEAN
5. SHE DOES NOT EAT THE TYRE

The answers are:

1. JE VOIS LE PONT MAIS PAS LA ROUTE ETROITE
2. ELLE A L'ESSENCE MAIS PAS L'HUILE
3. IL NE VOIT PAS LE CRIC
4. IL N'EST PAS JEUNE, MAIS JE NE SUIS PAS PROPRE
5. ELLE NE MANGE PAS LE PNEU

Now cover up the answers below and translate the following:

(You can write your answers in)

1. JE VEUX LE GARAGE, MAIS PAS LE BATEAU

2. VOUS NE MANGEZ PAS L'HUILE

3. JE MANGE L'OIE, MAIS VOUS NE MANGEZ PAS LA CHEVRE

4. IL VEUT L'ENTREE, MAIS ELLE NE VEUT PAS LA SORTIE

5. VOUS VOYEZ LE CHANGE, ET JE VOIS LA DOUANE

The answers are:

1. I WANT THE GARAGE BUT NOT THE BOAT

2. YOU DO NOT EAT THE OIL

3. I EAT THE GOOSE, BUT YOU DO NOT EAT THE GOAT

4. HE WANTS THE ENTRANCE, BUT SHE DOES NOT WANT THE EXIT

5. YOU SEE THE MONEY EXCHANGE, AND I SEE THE CUSTOMS

DAYS OF THE WEEK

THINK OF EACH IMAGE IN YOUR MIND'S EYE FOR ABOUT TEN SECONDS

○ The French for SUNDAY is DIMANCHE   (DEEMOnSH)
Imagine someone DEMANDS to see you on Sundays.

○ The French for MONDAY is LUNDI   (LenDEE)
Imagine your relatives LAND ON you on Mondays.

○ The French for TUESDAY is MARDI   (MARDEE)
Imagine MARDI GRAS, the carnival,
always takes place on Tuesdays.

○ The French for WEDNESDAY is   (MERKReDEE)
MERCREDI
Imagine Wednesdays is MARKET DAY.

○ The French for THURSDAY is JEUDI   (JeDEE)
Imagine you were sold SHODDY goods last Thursday.

○ The French for FRIDAY is VENDREDI   (VOnDReDEE)
Imagine Friday is the day you go for a little
WANDER IN town.

○ The French for SATURDAY is SAMEDI   (SAMDEE)
Imagine Saturdays always seem the same to
you SOMEDAYS.

YOU CAN WRITE YOUR ANSWERS IN

○ What is the English for SAMEDI?
  (SAMDEE)   _____

○ What is the English for VENDREDI?
  (VOnDReDee)   _____

○ What is the English for JEUDI? (JeDEE)   _____

○ What is the English for MERCREDI?
  (MERKReDEE)   _____

○ What is the English for MARDI?
  (MARDEE)   _____

○ What is the English for LUNDI? (LenDEE)   _____

○ What is the English for DIMANCHE?
  (DEEMOnSH)   _____

TURN BACK FOR THE ANSWERS

174

YOU CAN WRITE YOUR ANSWERS IN

○ What is the French for Saturday? _____

○ What is the French for Friday? _____

○ What is the French for Thursday? _____

○ What is the French for Wednesday? _____

○ What is the French for Tuesday? _____

○ What is the French for Monday? _____

○ What is the French for Sunday? _____

TURN BACK FOR THE ANSWERS

ELEMENTARY GRAMMAR
When you want to say: ON SATURDAY(S), etc., meaning every Saturday, you put LE (the) in front of the French word.

So,

ON SATURDAYS   is   LE SAMEDI

ON SATURDAYS I EAT   is   LE SAMEDI JE MANGE

Now cover up the answers below and translate the following:

(You can write your answers in)

1. ON SATURDAYS I AM TIRED
2. ON MONDAYS AND TUESDAYS I EAT IN A RESTAURANT
3. ON WEDNESDAYS, THURSDAYS AND SUNDAYS THE BOYS ARE DIRTY
4. ON FRIDAYS, THE DOG WANTS A DRINK
5. ON SUNDAYS, I SEE THE TOILET

The answers are:

1. LE SAMEDI JE SUIS FATIGUE
2. LE LUNDI ET LE MARDI JE MANGE DANS UN RESTAURANT
3. LE MERCREDI, LE JEUDI ET LE DIMANCHE LES GARÇONS SONT SALES
4. LE VENDREDI, LE CHIEN VEUT UNE BOISSON
5. LE DIMANCHE, JE VOIS LES TOILETTES

Now cover up the answers below and translate the following:

(You can write your answers in)

1. LE VENDREDI JE SUIS FATIGUE, MAIS LE DIMANCHE JE SUIS FACHE

2. LE MARDI VOUS VOYEZ LE DINER SUR LE PONT

3. LE MERCREDI ET LE LUNDI IL EST A LA PIECE

4. LE JEUDI VOUS MANGEZ DANS UN RESTAURANT, MAIS LE SAMEDI VOUS MANGEZ A LA PIECE

5. VOUS VOULEZ LES CHIENS LE JEUDI

The answers are:

1. ON FRIDAYS I AM TIRED, BUT ON SUNDAYS I AM ANGRY

2. ON TUESDAYS YOU SEE THE DINNER ON THE BRIDGE

3. ON WEDNESDAYS AND ON MONDAYS HE IS AT THE ROOM

4. ON THURSDAYS YOU EAT IN A RESTAURANT, BUT ON SATURDAYS YOU EAT AT THE ROOM

5. YOU WANT THE DOGS ON THURSDAYS

SOME MORE USEFUL VERBS

THINK OF EACH IMAGE IN YOUR MIND'S EYE FOR ABOUT TEN SECONDS

○ The French for I SPEAK is JE PARLE   (Je PARL)
Imagine an Indian Chief PARLEYING with a
cowboy — SPEAKING to him.

○ The French for I GO is JE VAIS   (Je VAY)
Imagine a German asking "Which VAY do I GO?"

○ The French for I SELL is JE VENDS   (Je VOn)
Imagine someone asking if you want to SELL
your VAN.

○ The French for I LIKE is J'AIME   (JEM)
Imagine saying "I do LIKE JAM."

YOU CAN WRITE YOUR ANSWERS IN

○ What is the English for J'AIME? (JEM)   _____

○ What is the English for JE VENDS?
(Je VOn)   _____

○ What is the English for JE VAIS? (Je VAY)   _____

○ What is the English for JE PARLE?
(Je PARL)   _____

TURN BACK FOR THE ANSWERS

YOU CAN WRITE YOUR ANSWERS IN

○ What is the French for I like?   _____

○ What is the French for I sell?   _____

○ What is the French for I go?   _____

○ What is the French for I speak?   _____

TURN BACK FOR THE ANSWERS

Now cover up the answers below and translate the following:

(You can write your answers in)

1. I SPEAK TO THE WIFE
2. I GO TO THE SUITCASE
3. I SELL THE TICKETS ON SUNDAYS
4. I LIKE THE GIRL BUT NOT THE BOY
5. I WANT THE POTATOES AND THE DRINKS

The answers are:

1. JE PARLE A LA FEMME
2. JE VAIS A LA VALISE
3. JE VENDS LES BILLETS LE DIMANCHE
4. J'AIME LA JEUNE FILLE MAIS PAS LE GARÇON
5. JE VEUX LES POMMES DE TERRE ET LES BOISSONS

Now cover up the answers below and translate the following:

(You can write your answers in)

1. JE PARLE SUR LE TOIT
2. JE VAIS A LA PORTE
3. JE NE VENDS PAS LES VACHES
4. J'AIME L'AUTO ROUGE
5. JE SUIS ASSEZ RAPIDE

The answers are:

1. I SPEAK ON THE ROOF
2. I GO TO THE DOOR
3. I DO NOT SELL THE COWS
4. I LIKE THE RED CAR
5. I AM QUITE QUICK

Section 9   ON THE BEACH AND LEISURE

THINK OF EACH IMAGE IN YOUR MIND'S EYE FOR ABOUT TEN SECONDS

○ The French for BEACH is PLAGE   (PLAJ)
  Imagine a PLAQUE on a Normandy beach,
  to commemorate the fighting.

○ The French for SEA is MER   (MER)
  Imagine a MARE and her foal plunging into the sea.

○ The French for SUN is SOLEIL   (SOLAY)
  Imagine it being very hot in the sun,
  SO LAY down and get a suntan.

○ The French for SAND is SABLE   (SABL)
  Imagine a SABLE skin coat, with sand on it.

○ The French for TOWEL is SERVIETTE   (SERVEE ET)
  Imagine using a SERVIETTE as a towel.

○ The French for PICNIC is PIQUE-NIQUE   (PEEK NEEK)
  Imagine taking a PICNIC to the Eiffel Tower.

○ The French for RIVER is RIVIERE   (REEVEE ER)
  Imagine a river flowing down to the RIVIERA.

○ The French for FOREST is FORET   (FORAY)
  Imagine going on a FORAY into the forest.

○ The French for COUNTRYSIDE is CAMPAGNE
  Imagine going with a COMPANION into the   (COnPANYe)
  countryside.

○ The French for MOUNTAIN is MONTAGNE   (MOHnTANYe)
  Imagine the Eiffel Tower on top of a MOUNTAIN.

YOU CAN WRITE YOUR ANSWERS IN

○ What is the English for MONTAGNE?
(MOHnTANYe)   _____

○ What is the English for CAMPAGNE?
(COnPANYe)   _____

○ What is the English for FOREST?
(FORAY)   _____

○ What is the English for RIVIERE?
(REEVEE ER)   _____

○ What is the English for PIQUE-NIQUE?
(PEEK NEEK)   _____

○ What is the English for SERVIETTE?
(SERVEE ET)   _____

○ What is the English for SABLE? (SABL)   _____

○ What is the English for SOLEIL? (SOLAY)   _____

○ What is the English for MER? (MER)   _____

○ What is the English for PLAGE? (PLAJ)   _____

TURN BACK FOR THE ANSWERS

THINK OF EACH IMAGE IN YOUR MIND'S EYE FOR ABOUT TEN SECONDS

○ The gender of BEACH is FEMININE   LA PLAGE
Imagine spraying a smelly beach with perfume.

○ The gender of SEA is FEMININE   LA MER
Imagine collecting sea water in perfume
bottles and selling it as perfume.

○ The gender of SUN is MASCULINE   LE SOLEIL
Imagine a boxer lying sunbathing in
the sun with his boxing gloves on.

○ The gender of SAND is MASCULINE   LE SABLE
Imagine a boxer falling onto a ring
covered in sand.

○ The gender of TOWEL is FEMININE   LA SERVIETTE
Imagine a towel smelling strongly of perfume.

○ The gender of PICNIC is MASCULINE   LE PIQUE-NIQUE
Imagine boxers sitting round eating a picnic.

○ The gender of RIVER is FEMININE   LA RIVIERE
Imagine a river of fragrant perfume.

○ The gender of FOREST is FEMININE   LA FORET
Imagine the perfume of pine needles in a forest.

○ The gender of COUNTRYSIDE is   LA CAMPAGNE
FEMININE
Imagine the smell of the countryside
captured in a new perfume.

○ The gender of MOUNTAIN is   LA MONTAGNE
FEMININE
Imagine a strong perfume coming off a
high mountain in the Alps.

YOU CAN WRITE YOUR ANSWERS IN

○ What is the gender and French for mountain? _____

○ What is the gender and French for countryside? _____

○ What is the gender and French for forest? _____

○ What is the gender and French for river? _____

○ What is the gender and French for picnic? _____

○ What is the gender and French for towel? _____

○ What is the gender and French for sand? _____

○ What is the gender and French for sun? _____

○ What is the gender and French for sea? _____

○ What is the gender and French for beach? _____

TURN BACK FOR THE ANSWERS

MORE LEISURE WORDS

THINK OF EACH IMAGE IN YOUR MIND'S EYE FOR ABOUT TEN SECONDS

○ The French for BOOK is LIVRE   (LEEVR)
Imagine putting a piece of LIVER on a book.

○ The French for LETTER is LETTRE   (LETR)
Imagine posting a LETTER from the Eiffel Tower.

○ The French for POSTAGE STAMP is TIMBRE   (TAHnBR)
Imagine a piece of TIMBER all covered in
postage stamps.

○ The French for NEWSPAPER is JOURNAL   (JOORNAL)
Imagine putting your newspaper inside a
heavy bound JOURNAL.

○ The French for CAMERA is APPAREIL   (APARAY)
Imagine your camera involves using elaborate
APPARATUS to take pictures.

○ The French for CAMERA FILM is   (PELEEKooL)
PELLICULE
Imagine using film wrapped round your
stomach to keep your BELLY COOL.

○ The French for THEATRE is THEATRE   (TAYATR)
Imagine having TEA AT the theatre.

○ The French for CINEMA is CINEMA   (SEENAYMA)
Imagine a CINEMA under the Eiffel Tower.

○ The French for (A) WALK is PROMENADE   (PROMNAD)
Imagine going for a walk along a seaside
PROMENADE.

○ The French for PEN is STYLO   (STEELOH)
Imagine a pen made from stainless STEEL, OH!

YOU CAN WRITE YOUR ANSWERS IN

○ What is the English for STYLO?
(STEELOH)   _____

○ What is the English for PROMENADE?
(PROMNAD)   _____

○ What is the English for CINEMA?
(SEENAYMA)   _____

○ What is the English for THEATRE?
(TAYATR)   _____

○ What is the English for PELLICULE?
(PELEEKooL)   _____

○ What is the English for APPAREIL?
(APARAY)   _____

○ What is the English for JOURNAL?
(JOORNAL)   _____

○ What is the English for TIMBRE?
(TAHnBR)   _____

○ What is the English for LETTRE? (LETR) _____

○ What is the English for LIVRE? (LEEVR) _____

TURN BACK FOR THE ANSWERS

THINK OF EACH IMAGE IN YOUR MIND'S EYE FOR ABOUT TEN SECONDS

○ The gender of BOOK is MASCULINE   LE LIVRE
Imagine a boxer reading a book before a fight.

○ The gender of LETTER is FEMININE   LA LETTRE
Imagine a perfumed letter from a lady friend.

○ The gender of POSTAGE STAMP is MASCULINE
Imagine a boxer covered in postage stamps.   LE TIMBRE

○ The gender of NEWSPAPER is MASCULINE
Imagine a boxer reading a newspaper   LE JOURNAL
before a fight.

○ The gender of CAMERA is MASCULINE   L'APPAREIL
Imagine photographers photographing
boxers during a fight.

○ The gender of CAMERA FILM is   LA PELLICULE
FEMININE
Imagine developing film by dipping it in perfume.

○ The gender of THEATRE is MASCULINE   LE THEATRE
Imagine watching a boxing match in a theatre.

○ The gender of CINEMA is MASCULINE   LE CINEMA
Imagine watching a film of a boxing
match in the cinema.

○ The gender of WALK is FEMININE   LA PROMENADE
Imagine finding bottles of perfume on your walk.

○ The gender of PEN is MASCULINE   LE STYLO
Imagine a boxer poking his opponent with a pen.

YOU CAN WRITE YOUR ANSWERS IN

○ What is the gender and French for pen? _____

○ What is the gender and French for a walk? _____

○ What is the gender and French for cinema? _____

○ What is the gender and French for theatre? _____

○ What is the gender and French for camera-film? _____

○ What is the gender and French for camera? _____

○ What is the gender and French for newspaper? _____

○ What is the gender and French for postage stamp? _____

○ What is the gender and French for letter? _____

○ What is the gender and French for book? _____

TURN BACK FOR THE ANSWERS

ELEMENTARY GRAMMAR

To make a word like "quickly" from "quick", or "quietly" from "quiet", you normally take the feminine form of the word and add MENT (MOn).

So,

QUICK   is RAPIDE

and QUICKLY   is RAPIDEMENT (RAPEEDMOn)

HEAVY   is LOURD

and HEAVILY   is LOURDEMENT (LOORDMOn)

Now cover up the answers below and translate the following:

(You can write your answers in)

1. ON TUESDAYS I EAT THE PICNIC QUIETLY
2. SHE WANTS THE RED POSTAGE STAMP QUICKLY
3. HE WAS STUPIDLY DIRTY AT TEN PAST THREE
4. SHE WANTS A NEWSPAPER QUICKLY AT THE TABLE
5. HE EATS QUIETLY IN THE ROOM

The answers are:

1. LE MARDI JE MANGE LE PIQUE-NIQUE TRAN-QUILLEMENT
2. ELLE VEUT LE TIMBRE ROUGE RAPIDEMENT
3. IL ETAIT STUPIDEMENT SALE A TROIS HEURES DIX
4. ELLE VEUT UN JOURNAL RAPIDEMENT A LA TABLE
5. IL MANGE TRANQUILLEMENT DANS LA PIECE

Now cover up the answers below and translate the following:

(You can write your answers in)

1. IL MANGE LA VACHE RAPIDEMENT
2. ELLE MANGE LES POMMES DE TERRE
   TRANQUILLEMENT
3. VOUS MANGEZ STUPIDEMENT
4. VOUS VOULEZ LA PLAGE RAPIDEMENT
5. JE PARLE TRANQUILLEMENT A LA RIVIERE

The answers are:

1. HE EATS THE COW QUICKLY
2. SHE EATS THE POTATOES QUIETLY
3. YOU EAT STUPIDLY
4. YOU WANT THE BEACH QUICKLY
5. I SPEAK QUIETLY TO THE RIVER

SOME MORE USEFUL WORDS

THINK OF EACH IMAGE IN YOUR MIND'S EYE FOR ABOUT TEN SECONDS

○ The French for HOUSE is MAISON   (MAYZOHn)
Imagine a stone-MASON cleaning your house.

○ The French for POLICE is POLICE   (POLEES)
Imagine the POLICE surrounding the Eiffel Tower.

○ The French for CHEMIST'S SHOP is   (FARMASEE)
PHARMACIE
Imagine the PHARMACY in your local chemist's shop.

○ The French for BANK is BANQUE   (BOnK)
Imagine a BANK at the top of the Eiffel Tower.

○ The French for HOTEL is HOTEL   (OTEL)
Imagine staying at an HOTEL in the Eiffel Tower.

○ The French for INN is AUBERGE   (OBERJ)
Imagine piles of AUBERGINES at the
door of an inn.

○ The French for MARKET is MARCHE   (MARSHAY)
Imagine MARCHING through a market.

○ The French for BAKER'S SHOP is   (BOOLOnJeREE)
BOULANGERIE
Imagine that in France, baker's shops
sell bread and underwear for
bulls — BULL LINGERIE. Sometimes
the bread is wrapped in bull's lingerie.

○ The French for BUTCHER'S SHOP is   (BOOSHeREE)
BOUCHERIE
Imagine a BUTCHER'S SHOP beside the Eiffel Tower.

○ The French for STATION is GARE   (GAR)
Imagine parking your CAR at the station.

YOU CAN WRITE YOUR ANSWERS IN

○ What is the English for GARE? (GAR) _____

○ What is the English for BOUCHERIE?
(BOOSHeREE) _____

○ What is the English for BOULANGERIE?
(BOOLOnJeREE) _____

○ What is the English for MARCHE?
(MARSHAY) _____

○ What is the English for AUBERGE?
(OBERJ) _____

○ What is the English for HOTEL? (OTEL) _____

○ What is the English for BANQUE? (BOnK) _____

○ What is the English for PHARMACIE?
(FARMASEE) _____

○ What is the English for POLICE?
(POLEES) _____

○ What is the English for MAISON?
(MAYZOHn) _____

TURN BACK FOR THE ANSWERS

THINK OF EACH IMAGE IN YOUR MIND'S EYE FOR ABOUT TEN SECONDS

○ The gender of HOUSE is FEMININE   LA MAISON
  Imagine spraying perfume throughout
  your house to stop a nasty smell.

○ The gender of POLICE is FEMININE   LA POLICE
  Imagine the police spraying
  themselves with perfume.

○ The gender of CHEMIST'S SHOP is   LA PHARMACIE
  FEMININE
  Imagine buying perfume in a chemist's shop.

○ The gender of BANK is FEMININE   LA BANQUE
  Imagine trying to lodge a bottle of
  perfume in your bank account.

○ The gender of HOTEL is MASCULINE   L'HOTEL
  Imagine your hotel is full of boxers.

○ The gender of INN is FEMININE   L'AUBERGE
  Imagine a strong smell of perfume at
  the small inn you are staying at.

○ The gender of MARKET is MASCULINE   LE MARCHE
  Imagine boxers milling round a market.

○ The gender of BAKER'S SHOP is   LA BOULANGERIE
  FEMININE
  Imagine a baker's shop smelling
  beautifully of perfume.

○ The gender of BUTCHER'S SHOP is   LA BOUCHERIE
  FEMININE
  Imagine a butcher's shop giving
  bottles of perfume free with lumps of meat.

○ The gender of STATION is FEMININE   LA GARE
  Imagine bottles of perfume stacked on
  a station platform.

YOU CAN WRITE YOUR ANSWERS IN

○ What is the gender and French for station? _____

○ What is the gender and French for butcher's shop? _____

○ What is the gender and French for baker's shop? _____

○ What is the gender and French for market? _____

○ What is the gender and French for inn? _____

○ What is the gender and French for hotel? _____

○ What is the gender and French for bank? _____

○ What is the gender and French for chemist's shop? _____

○ What is the gender and French for police? _____

○ What is the gender and French for house? _____

TURN BACK FOR THE ANSWERS

ELEMENTARY GRAMMAR

In French, words like MY, HIS, etc. have two forms: one in the masculine and one in the feminine.

For example,

    THE DOG   is MON CHIEN (MOHn)

    MY TABLE is MA TABLE (MA)

In other words, the MY is masculine if it goes with a masculine word, but it is feminine if it goes with a feminine word.

So,

MY DOG IS BLACK   is MON CHIEN EST NOIR
                             (masculine)

MY TABLE IS BLACK is MA TABLE EST NOIRE (feminine)

  To remember that MY is MON:

  Imagine thinking "MY doesn't HE MOAN!"

  To remember that MY is MA:

  Imagine thinking "SHE is MY MA."

The same rule is also true for HIS.

  The French for HIS is SON (SOHn).

  Imagine him singing HIS SONG.

The French for HIS when it goes with a feminine word is SA (SA).
  Imagine his SIghing at a beautiful girl.

So,

HIS DOG IS BLACK   is SON CHIEN EST NOIR
                             (masculine)

HIS TABLE IS BLACK is SA TABLE EST NOIRE (feminine)

You must remember that HIS is feminine when it is used with a feminine noun. Similarly, the word HER is masculine when it goes with a masculine noun.

So, the French for HER is also SON when it goes with a masculine noun, and SA when it goes with a feminine noun.

So,

HER DOG IS BLACK   is SON CHIEN EST NOIR

HER TABLE IS BLACK is SA TABLE EST NOIRE

ITS is also the same as HIS and HER.

So,

ITS DOG IS BLACK   is SON CHIEN EST NOIR

ITS TABLE IS BLACK is SA TABLE EST NOIRE

Now cover up the answers below and translate the following:

(You can write your answers in)

1. MY SAND IS HARD AND DRY
2. HIS TOWEL AND HIS PICNIC WERE DIRTY
3. HER MOUNTAIN IS VERY PRETTY, BUT HER CUPBOARD IS DRY
4. MY FOREST IS GREEN
5. HER TOWEL IS QUITE SHORT

The answers are:

1. MON SABLE EST DUR ET SEC
2. SA SERVIETTE ET SON PIQUE-NIQUE ETAIENT SALES
3. SA MONTAGNE EST TRES JOLIE, MAIS SON PLACARD EST SEC
4. MA FORET EST VERTE
5. SA SERVIETTE EST ASSEZ COURTE

ELEMENTARY GRAMMAR

The French for YOUR is VOTRE (pronounced VOTR)

Imagine you are a VOTER for YOUR candidate.

The French for OUR is NOTRE (pronounced NOTR)

Remember, NOTRE Dame is the church of OUR Lady.

This is the same for masculine and feminine words.

Now cover up the answers below and translate the following:

(You can write your answers in)

1. YOUR SAND IS DIRTY
2. OUR TOWEL IS WHITE
3. YOUR MOUNTAIN IS HEAVY
4. OUR PICNIC IS SMALL
5. MY HORSE IS BLACK

The answers are:

1. VOTRE SABLE EST SALE
2. NOTRE SERVIETTE EST BLANCHE
3. VOTRE MONTAGNE EST LOURDE
4. NOTRE PIQUE-NIQUE EST PETIT
5. MON CHEVAL EST NOIR

In the following translations, you can use the word HIS for HER, and HER for HIS throughout. Cover up the answers below.

You can write your answers in.

1. MON MARCHE EST SUR LE PONT

2. MA BANQUE ET MA GARE SONT NOIRES

3. SON HOTEL ET SON LIVRE SONT SALES, MAIS SA LETTRE ET SA MERE SONT PROPRES

4. SON STYLO ET SON APPAREIL ETAIENT ROUGES, MAIS SA PELLICULE ET SA PIECE ETAIENT JAUNES

5. VOTRE BOULANGERIE ET VOTRE BOUCHERIE SONT PLEINES, MAIS NOTRE TIMBRE ET NOTRE JOURNAL SONT BLANCS

The answers are:

1. MY MARKET IS ON THE BRIDGE

2. MY BANK AND MY STATION ARE BLACK

3. HIS HOTEL AND HIS BOOK ARE DIRTY, BUT HIS LETTER AND HIS MOTHER ARE CLEAN

4. HER PEN AND HER CAMERA WERE RED, BUT HER --CAMERA FILM AND HER ROOM WERE YELLOW

5. YOUR BAKER'S SHOP AND YOUR BUTCHER'S SHOP ARE FULL, BUT OUR STAMP AND OUR NEWSPAPER ARE WHITE

ELEMENTARY GRAMMAR
You have just seen that MY, HIS, HER are masculine or feminine, depending on the word they go with.

This is very tricky and you will make mistakes.

Another slight complication is that the words for MY, etc., change if the word they go with is plural.

So,

MY DOGS is MES CHIENS (MAY)

Imagine saying "MAY I see MY dogs?"

YOUR DOGS is VOS CHIENS (VO)

Imagine your VOtes are here.

HIS DOGS   is SES CHIENS (SAY)
HER DOGS is SES CHIENS

Imagine saying "Where are HIS/HER dogs?"

OUR DOGS is NOS CHIENS (NO)

Imagine a Scot saying "It's NO our dogs."

So,

MY	is	MON, MA or MES
HIS or HER	is	SON, SA or SES
YOUR	is	VOTRE or VOS
OUR	is	NOTRE or NOS

For example,

OUR HOTELS ARE DIRTY is NOS HOTELS SONT SALES

YOUR BANKS ARE CLEAN is VOS BANQUES SONT PROPRES

Now cover up the answers below and translate the following:

(You can write your answers in)

1. OUR CHEMIST'S SHOPS ARE FULL
2. I EAT YOUR CHICKENS AND YOUR HEDGEHOGS
3. SHE WANTS HER CARS
4. OUR PENS ARE COLD AND GREEN
5. HIS CAMERA FILMS ARE UNDER THE BLACK HOUSE

The answers are:

1. NOS PHARMACIES SONT PLEINES
2. JE MANGE VOS POULES ET VOS HERISSONS
3. ELLE VEUT SES AUTOS
4. NOS STYLOS SONT FROIDS ET VERTS
5. SES PELLICULES SONT SOUS LA MAISON NOIRE

Now cover up the answers below and translate the following:

(You can write your answers in)

1. MES MAISONS SONT SALES, ET VOS GARES SONT SALES, MAIS SES HOTELS NE SONT PAS SALES

2. NOS SERVIETTES SONT SECHES ET VOS TIMBRES SONT ETROITS, MAIS SES JOURNAUX SONT DURS

3. MA CAMPAGNE EST NOIRE, ET VOS RIVIERES SONT SALES, MAIS NOTRE MONTAGNE EST VERTE

4. VOTRE BANQUE EST SALE ET VOS HOTELS SONT PLEINS, MAIS NOS AUBERGES SONT PROPRES

5. NOS CHIENS SONT LOURDS, VOTRE CHIEN EST SEC, MA CHEVRE EST TRES TRANQUILLE ET SA VACHE EST MINCE

The answers are:

1. MY HOUSES ARE DIRTY, AND YOUR STATIONS ARE DIRTY, BUT HIS HOTELS ARE NOT DIRTY

2. OUR TOWELS ARE DRY AND YOUR STAMPS ARE NARROW, BUT HER NEWSPAPERS ARE HARD

3. MY COUNTRYSIDE IS BLACK, AND YOUR RIVERS ARE DIRTY, BUT OUR MOUNTAIN IS GREEN

4. YOUR BANK IS DIRTY AND YOUR HOTELS ARE FULL, BUT OUR INNS ARE CLEAN

5. OUR DOGS ARE HEAVY, YOUR DOG IS DRY, MY GOAT IS VERY QUIET AND HIS COW IS THIN

Section 10 AT THE DOCTOR'S, EMERGENCY WORDS, USEFUL WORDS

AT THE DOCTOR'S

THINK OF EACH IMAGE IN YOUR MIND'S EYE FOR ABOUT TEN SECONDS

○ The French for PAIN is DOULEUR   (DOOLeR)
Imagine being given a DOLLAR to make your
pain go away.

○ The French for ILLNESS is MALADIE   (MALADEE)
Imagine thinking your friend is looking very
ill — he has some MALADY.

○ The French for MOUTH is BOUCHE   (BOOSH)
Imagine a BUSH growing out of your mouth.

○ The French for ARM is BRAS   (BRA)
Imagine a lady's BRA strapped round your arm.

○ The French for LEG is JAMBE   (JOnB)
Imagine JAM spread all over your leg.

○ The French for THROAT is GORGE   (GORJ)
Imagine your GORGE a huge meal which
sticks in your throat.

○ The French for BACK is DOS   (DOH)
Imagine making DOUGH on your mother's back.

○ The French for HAND is MAIN   (MAHn)
Imagine a MAN waving his hand.

○ The French for RIB is COTE   (KOT)
Imagine wrapping a rib in a COAT.

○ The French for TONGUE is LANGUE   (LOnG)
Imagine sticking out a very LONG tongue.

YOU CAN WRITE YOUR ANSWERS IN

○ What is the English for LANGUE? (LOnG) _____

○ What is the English for COTE? (KOT) _____

○ What is the English for MAIN? (MAHn) _____

○ What is the English for DOS? (DOH) _____

○ What is the English for GORGE? (GORJ) _____

○ What is the English for JAMBE? (JOnB) _____

○ What is the English for BRAS? (BRA) _____

○ What is the English for BOUCHE?
(BOOSH) _____

○ What is the English for MALADIE?
(MALADEE) _____

○ What is the English for DOULEUR?
(DOOLeR) _____

TURN BACK FOR THE ANSWERS

THINK OF EACH IMAGE IN YOUR MIND'S EYE FOR ABOUT TEN SECONDS

○ The gender of PAIN is FEMININE   LA DOULEUR
   Imagine squirting perfume on a painful spot.

○ The gender of ILLNESS is FEMININE   LA MALADIE
   Imagine spraying perfume round a room
   where there is illness.

○ The gender of MOUTH is FEMININE   LA BOUCHE
   Imagine spraying your mouth with perfume
   after drinking too much.

○ The gender of ARM is MASCULINE   LE BRAS
   Imagine a boxer testing his arm for strength.

○ The gender of LEG is FEMININE   LA JAMBE
   Imagine a lady spraying her leg with perfume.

○ The gender of THROAT is FEMININE   LA GORGE
   Imagine spraying the back of your sore
   throat with perfume.

○ The gender of BACK is MASCULINE   LE DOS
   Imagine a boxer lying flat on his back.

○ The gender of HAND is FEMININE   LA MAIN
   Imagine washing your hands in perfume.

○ The gender of RIB is FEMININE   LA COTE
   Imagine cooking spare ribs in a perfume sauce.

○ The gender of TONGUE is FEMININE   LA LANGUE
   Imagine putting a small bit of perfume on
   your tongue to taste it.

YOU CAN WRITE YOUR ANSWERS IN

○ What is the gender and French for tongue? _____

○ What is the gender and French for rib? _____

○ What is the gender and French for hand? _____

○ What is the gender and French for back? _____

○ What is the gender and French for throat? _____

○ What is the gender and French for leg? _____

○ What is the gender and French for arm? _____

○ What is the gender and French for mouth? _____

○ What is the gender and French for illness? _____

○ What is the gender and French for pain? _____

TURN BACK FOR THE ANSWERS

SOME EMERGENCY AND USEFUL WORDS

THINK OF EACH IMAGE IN YOUR MIND'S EYE FOR ABOUT TEN SECONDS

○ The French for DANGER is DANGER (DOnJAY)
Imagine a notice on the Eiffel Tower:
"DANGER, do not lean over."

○ The French for BLOOD is SANG (SOn)
Imagine someone who sang a SONG as
blood came out of his mouth.

○ The French for FIRE! is AU FEU! (OH Fe)
Imagine feeling AWFUL because you are
caught in a fire.

○ The French for AMBULANCE is (OnBooLOnS)
AMBULANCE
Imagine AMBULANCES racing to the Eiffel Tower.

○ The French for HELP! is AU SECOURS! (OH SKOOR)
Imagine OSCAR Wilde shouting for help.

○ The French for HOSPITAL is HOPITAL (OPEETAL)
Imgine the Eiffel Tower converted into a HOSPITAL.

○ The French for THIEF is VOLEUR (VOLeR)
Imagine shouting "FOLLOW that thief."

○ The French for TELEPHONE is (TAYLAYFON)
TELEPHONE
Imagine throwing TELEPHONES from the
top of the Eiffel Tower.

○ The French for DOCTOR is MEDECIN (MAYDSAHn)
Imagine a doctor giving you MEDICINE.

○ The French for DENTIST is DENTISTE (DOnTEEST)
Imagine a DENTIST taking your teeth out
in the Eiffel Tower.

YOU CAN WRITE YOUR ANSWERS IN

○ What is the English for DENTISTE?
(DOnTEEST)   _____

○ What is the English for MEDECIN?
(MAYDSAHn)   _____

○ What is the English for TELEPHONE?
(TAYLAYFON)   _____

○ What is the English for VOLEUR? (VOLeR)   _____

○ What is the English for HOPITAL?
(OPEETAL)   _____

○ What is the English for AU SECOURS!?
(OH SKOOR)   _____

○ What is the English for AMBULANCE?
(OnBooLOnS)   _____

○ What is the English for AU FEU! (OH Fe)   _____

○ What is the English for SANG? (SOn)   _____

○ What is the English for DANGER?
(DOnJAY)   _____

TURN BACK FOR THE ANSWERS

THINK OF EACH IMAGE IN YOUR MIND'S EYE FOR ABOUT TEN SECONDS

○ The gender of DANGER is MASCULINE
Imagine shouting to a boxer "Danger,   (LE DANGER)
watch your head."

○ The gender of BLOOD is MASCULINE   (LE SANG)
Imagine blood coming from a boxer's face.

○ The gender of AMBULANCE is   (L'AMBULANCE)
FEMININE
Imagine fumigating an ambulance with perfume.

○ The gender of HOSPITAL is MASCULINE   (L'HOPITAL)
Imagine carting a boxer off to hospital.

○ The gender of THIEF is MASCULINE   (LE VOLEUR)
Imagine a thief stealing a boxer's clothes
while he is boxing.

○ The gender of TELEPHONE is   (LE TELEPHONE)
MASCULINE
Imagine telephoning a boxer to tell him not to fight.

○ The gender of DOCTOR is MASCULINE   (LE MEDECIN)
Imagine a doctor looking at a boxer after
he has been knocked out.

○ The gender of DENTIST is MASCULINE   (LE DENTISTE)
Imagine taking a boxer to a dentist after
he has had his teeth knocked out.

PLEASE NOTE: FIRE! and HELP! have no gender

217

YOU CAN WRITE YOUR ANSWERS IN

○ What is the gender and French for dentist? _____

○ What is the gender and French for doctor? _____

○ What is the gender and French for telephone? _____

○ What is the gender and French for thief? _____

○ What is the gender and French for hospital? _____

○ What is the gender and French for ambulance? _____

○ What is the gender and French for blood? _____

○ What is the gender and French for danger? _____

TURN BACK FOR THE ANSWERS

ELEMENTARY GRAMMAR

When you want to say things like THE BOY'S BOOK, in French you must say THE BOOK OF THE BOY, and so on.

The word for OF is DE (pronounced De).

Imagine thinking that this is the book OF DE boy.

To say OF THE you say DE LA if the word following is feminine.

So,

OF THE MEAT   is DE LA VIANDE

OF THE MOUTH is DE LA BOUCHE

If the word is masculine, OF THE is DU (pronounced Doo).

Imagine asking "DO you have to say OF THE?"

So,

OF THE DOG is DU CHIEN

OF THE ARM is DU BRAS

Also, of course:

THE BOY'S MOUTH   is THE MOUTH OF THE BOY (LA BOUCHE DU GARCON)

THE GIRL'S ARM   is THE ARM OF THE GIRL (LE BRAS DE LA JEUNE FILLE)

Now cover up the answers below and translate the following:

(You can write your answers in)

1. THE BOY'S FATHER IS BLACK
2. THE MOTHER'S TONGUE IS NARROW, AND THE FATHER'S BLOOD IS RED
3. THE THIEF'S KNIFE IS VERY BIG
4. THE DOCTOR'S HOUSE AND THE DENTIST'S MOUTH ARE VERY DRY
5. THE BOY'S LEG IS SHORT BUT CLEAN

The answers are:

1. LE PERE DU GARÇON EST NOIR
2. LA LANGUE DE LA MERE EST ETROITE, ET LE SANG DU PERE EST ROUGE
3. LE COUTEAU DU VOLEUR EST TRES GRAND
4. LA MAISON DU MEDECIN ET LA BOUCHE DU DENTISTE SONT TRES SECHES
5. LA JAMBE DU GARÇON EST COURTE MAIS PROPRE

Now cover up the answers below and translate the following:

(You can write your answers in)

1. LE BRAS DU GARÇON EST BON

2. LA DOULEUR DU MARI EST ICI, PAS LA

3. LA MALADIE DE LA SOEUR N'EST PAS BONNE

4. LA COTE DE MON FRERE ET LA GORGE DE MA MERE
   SONT TRES ETROITES

5. LE DOS DE VOTRE JEUNE FILLE ET LA MAIN DE
   NOTRE FILS ETAIENT ASSEZ NOIRS

The answers are:

1. THE BOY'S ARM IS GOOD

2. THE HUSBAND'S PAIN IS HERE, NOT THERE

3. THE SISTER'S ILLNESS IS NOT GOOD

4. MY BROTHER'S RIB AND MY MOTHER'S THROAT ARE
   VERY NARROW

5. YOUR GIRL'S BACK AND OUR SON'S HAND WERE
   QUITE BLACK

ANOTHER GROUP OF USEFUL WORDS

THINK OF EACH IMAGE IN YOUR MIND'S EYE FOR ABOUT TEN SECONDS

○ The French for LEFT is GAUCHE   (GOSH)
Imagine thinking "GOSH, I'm left-handed."

○ The French for RIGHT is DROITE   (DRWAT)
Imagine you having to DRAW IT with your right hand.

○ The French for TOWN is VILLE   (VEEL)
Imagine you own a VILLA in the centre of town.

○ The French for RAIN is PLUIE   (PLWEE)
Imagine telling your children to go and PLAY in the rain.

○ The French for SNOW is NEIGE   (NEJ)
Imagine a horse which NEIGHS every time it snows.

○ The French for ICE is GLACE   (GLAS)
Imagine a sheet of ice looking like GLASS.
(GLACE is also the French for ICE CREAM.)

YOU CAN WRITE YOUR ANSWERS IN

○ What is the English for GLACE? (GLAS) _____

○ What is the English for NEIGE? (NEJ) _____

○ What is the English for PLUIE? (PLWEE) _____

○ What is the English for VILLE? (VEEL) _____

○ What is the English for DROITE?
   (DRWAT) _____

○ What is the English for GAUCHE? (GOSH) _____

TURN BACK FOR THE ANSWERS

THINK OF EACH IMAGE IN YOUR MIND'S EYE FOR ABOUT TEN SECONDS

○ The gender of LEFT is FEMININE   LA GAUCHE
  Imagine spraying perfume to the left.

○ The gender of RIGHT is FEMININE   LA DROITE
  Imagine spraying perfume to the right.

○ The gender of TOWN is FEMININE   LA VILLE
  Imagine a town that sells nothing but perfume.

○ The gender of RAIN is FEMININE   LA PLUIE
  Imagine rain that smells of perfume.

○ The gender of SNOW is FEMININE   LA NEIGE
  Imagine spraying snow with perfume to make it melt.

○ The gender of ICE is FEMININE   LA GLACE
  Imagine trying to make ice by spraying it with perfume.

YOU CAN WRITE YOUR ANSWERS IN

○ What is the gender and French for ice? _____

○ What is the gender and French for snow? _____

○ What is the gender and French for rain? _____

○ What is the gender and French for town? _____

○ What is the gender and French for right? _____

○ What is the gender and French for left? _____

TURN BACK FOR THE ANSWERS

SOME MORE USEFUL WORDS

THINK OF EACH IMAGE IN YOUR MIND'S EYE FOR ABOUT TEN SECONDS

○ The French for SLOW is LENT   (LOn)
  Imagine being told "Go SLOW for a LONG time."

○ The French for WET is MOUILLE   (MOO YAY)
  Imagine Moses saying to cows
  "MOO! YEH, even in the WET."

○ The French for ENGAGED is OCCUPE   (OKooPAY)
  Imagine the toilet being ENGAGED
  because someone is OCCUPYING it.

○ The French for CLOSED is FERME   (FERMAY)
  Imagine something being CLOSED FOR ME.

○ The French for PLEASE is
  S'IL VOUS PLAIT   (SEEL VOO PLAY)
  Imagine saying "PLEASE can I have a
  SILVER PLATE."

○ The French for THANK YOU is MERCI   (MERSEE)
  Imagine THANKING someone for the
  MERCY he has shown you.

YOU CAN WRITE YOUR ANSWERS IN

○ What is the English for MERCI?
(MERSEE)   _____

○ What is the English for S'IL VOUS
PLAIT? (SEEL VOO PLAY)   _____

○ What is the English for FERME?
(FERMAY)   _____

○ What is the English for OCCUPE?
(OKooPAY)   _____

○ What is the English for MOUILLE?
(MOO YAY)   _____

○ What is the English for LENT? (LOn)   _____

TURN BACK FOR THE ANSWERS

YOU CAN WRITE YOUR ANSWERS IN

○ What is the French for thank you?   _____

○ What is the French for please?   _____

○ What is the French for closed?   _____

○ What is the French for engaged?   _____

○ What is the French for wet?   _____

○ What is the French for slow?   _____

TURN BACK FOR THE ANSWERS

ELEMENTARY GRAMMAR

When you want to say OF THE AMBULANCE, you say DE L'AMBULANCE.

In other words, for words which begin with a vowel in French, you always say DE L' when you mean OF THE.

Finally when the word is plural, such as OF THE DOGS, then the word for OF THE is DES (pronounced DAY), whether it is masculine or feminine.

So,

OF THE DOGS is DES CHIENS

PLEASE NOTE:

I SELL and I AM SELLING,

I SEE and I AM SEEING

are translated in the same way, since in French they are the same.

Now cover up the answers below and translate the following:

(You can write your answers in)

1. THE AMBULANCE'S TYRE IS VERY NARROW
2. THE DOGS OF THE TOWN ARE VERY DIRTY
3. I LIKE THE COLD RAIN, I SELL THE DRY ICE
4. I SPEAK VERY SLOWLY, I AM GOING VERY QUICKLY
5. I AM SELLING THE VERY WHITE WINE

The answers are:

1. LE PNEU DE L'AMBULANCE EST TRES ETROIT
2. LES CHIENS DE LA VILLE SONT TRES SALES
3. J'AIME LA PLUIE FROIDE, JE VENDS LA GLACE SECHE
4. JE PARLE TRES LENTEMENT, JE VAIS TRES
   RAPIDEMENT
5. JE VENDS LE VIN TRES BLANC*

*Adjectives which go in front of the noun usually go after it when used with.

MONTHS OF THE YEAR

With the possible exceptions of July and August, the months of the year are quite similar in French and English, so images will be given only for July and August.

The French for JULY is JUILLET

(pronounced JWEEYAY)

Imagine July is WEARYING.

The French for AUGUST is AOUT

(pronounced OOT)

Imagine the owl begins to HOOT in August.

THE MONTHS OF THE YEAR

English	French	Pronounced
January	JANVIER	JOnVEE AY
February	FEVRIER	FAYVREE AY
March	MARS	MARS
April	AVRIL	AVREEL
May	MAI	MAY
June	JUIN	JWAHn
July	JUILLET	JWEEYAY
August	AOUT	OOT
September	SEPTEMBRE	SEPTOnBR
October	OCTOBRE	OKTOBR
November	NOVEMBRE	NOVOnBR
December	DECEMBRE	DAYSOnBR

If you want to say IN JANUARY, etc.,

you say EN JANVIER, etc.

Now cover up the answers below and translate the following:

(You can write your answers in)

1. I EAT THE MEAT IN SEPTEMBER BUT NOT IN OCTOBER
2. I WAS ILL IN AUGUST AND I WAS STUPID IN JULY
3. THE BLUE HEDGEHOG HAS SEVEN BOYS IN JANUARY
4. I HAVE THE PAIN IN MARCH AND IN APRIL
5. MY MOUTH WAS RED IN DECEMBER

The answers are:

1. JE MANGE LA VIANDE EN SEPTEMBRE MAIS PAS EN OCTOBRE
2. J'ETAIS MALADE EN AOUT ET J'ETAIS STUPIDE EN JUILLET
3. LE HERISSON BLEU A SEPT GARÇONS EN JANVIER
4. J'AI LA DOULEUR EN MARS ET EN AVRIL
5. MA BOUCHE ETAIT ROUGE EN DECEMBRE

Now cover up the answers below and translate the following:

(You can write your answers in)

1. AU SECOURS! L'ARGENT DE LA BANQUE EST SALE. OU EST LE TELEPHONE, S'IL VOUS PLAIT?

2. MERCI. JE VOIS LA NEIGE BLANCHE MAIS PAS LA PLUIE MOUILLEE

3. DANGER! AU FEU! LA MAISON DES VOLEURS EST ROUGE

4. LES TOILETTES DU HERISSON SONT OCCUPEES

5. L'ESSENCE DE L'AMBULANCE EST BLEUE

The answers are:

1. HELP! THE BANK'S MONEY IS DIRTY. WHERE IS THE TELEPHONE, PLEASE?

2. THANK YOU. I SEE THE WHITE SNOW BUT NOT THE WET RAIN

3. DANGER! FIRE! THE THIEVES' HOUSE IS RED

4. THE HEDGEHOG'S TOILET(S) IS (ARE) ENGAGED

5. THE AMBULANCE'S PETROL IS BLUE

This is the end of the course. We hope you have enjoyed it! Of course words and grammar will not be remembered for ever without revision, but if you look at the book from time to time, you will be surprised at how quickly everything comes back.

When you go abroad, do not be too shy to try out what you have learnt. Your host will appreciate your making the effort to speak, even if you sometimes make mistakes. And the more you attempt to speak the more you will learn!

GLOSSARY

a (an)	un/une	ceiling	le plafond
accountant	le comptable	chair	la chaise
am	suis	cheese	le fromage
ambulance	l'ambulance (f)	chemist's shop	la pharmacie
and	et	cheque	le chèque
angry	fâché	cinema	le cinéma
animal	l'animal (m)	clean	propre
apple	la pomme	clock	la pendule
are (you)	êtes	closed	fermé
are (they)	sont	clothes	les vêtements (m)
arm	le bras		
armchair	le fauteuil	coffee	le café
at	à	cold	froid
back	le dos	contract	le contrat
baker's shop	la boulangerie	countryside	la campagne
bank	la banque	cow	la vache
beach	la plage	cup	la tasse
bean	le haricot	cupboard	le placard
because	parce que	curtain	le rideau
bed	le lit	customs	la douane
beer	la bière	cutlery	le couvert
big	grand	danger	le danger
bill	l'addition (f)	daughter	la fille
black	noir	day	le jour
blood	le sang	dear	le cerf
blue	bleu	deep	profond
boat	le bateau	dentist	le dentiste
book	le livre	difficult	difficile
boss	le patron	dinner	le dîner
boy	le garçon	dirty	sale
bread	le pain	doctor	le médecin
bridge	le pont	dog	le chien
brother	le frère	door	la porte
but	mais	dress	la robe
butcher's shop	la boucherie	drink	la boisson
butter	le beurre	dry	sec (sèche)
cabbage	le chou	duck	le canard
camera	l'appareil (m)	easy	facile
camera film	la pellicule	eat (I)	mange
car	l'auto (f)	eat (they)	mangent
carpet	le tapis	eat (you)	mangez
cash till	la caisse	eats	mange
cat	le chat	egg	l'oeuf (m)

elephant	l'éléphant (m)	high	haut
empty	vide	his	son/sa/ses
engaged	occupé	holidays	les vacances (f)
entrance	l'entrée (f)	horse	le cheval
exit	la sortie	hospital	l'hôpital (m)
expensive	cher	hot	chaud
factory	l'usine (f)	hotel	l'hôtel (m)
father	le père	hour	l'heure (f)
fire!	au feu!	house	la maison
firm	la compagnie	how	comment
fish	le poisson	husband	le mari
floor	le plancher	I	je
flower	la fleur	ice	la glace
fly	la mouche	ice cream	la glace
food	la nourriture	illness	la maladie
forest	la forêt	in	dans
fork	la fourchette	inn	l'auberge (f)
fruit	le fruit	insect	l'insecte (m)
full	plein	is	est
garage	le garage	its	son/sa/ses
garden	le jardin	jack	le cric
garlic	l'aïl (m)	jacket	la veste
girl	la jeune fille	key	la clef
glass	le verre	kitchen	la cuisine
go (I)	vais	knife	le couteau
goat	la chèvre	left	la gauche
gold(en)	doré	leg	la jambe
good	bon	letter	la lettre
goose	l'oie (f)	lettuce	la salade
grass	l'herbe (f)	like (I)	aime
green	vert	lobster	le homard
grey	gris	lunch	le déjeuner
half (of time)	demie	manager	le directeur
hand	la main	market	le marché
hard	dur	meat	la viande
has	a	menu	la carte
hat	le chapeau	midday	midi
have (I)	ai	midnight	minuit
have (they)	ont	milk	le lait
have (you)	avez	minute	la minute
he	il	mistake	l'erreur (f)
heavy	lourd	money	l'argent (m)
hedgehog	le hérisson	money	
help!	au secours!	exchange	le change
hen	la poule	month	le mois
her	son/sa/ses	morning	le matin
here	ici	mother	la mère

237

mountain	la montagne	restaurant	le restaurant
mouse	la souris	rib	la côte
mouth	la bouche	right	la droite
mushroom	le champignon	river	la rivière
my	mon/ma/mes	road	la route
narrow	étroit	roof	le toit
newspaper	le journal	room	la pièce
night	la nuit	salary	le salaire
no	non	salesman	le vendeur
not	pas	sand	le sable
of the	du/de la/des	sea	la mer
office	le bureau	second	la seconde
oil	l'huile (f)	secretary	la secrétaire
on	sur	see (I)	vois
or	ou	see (they)	voient
orange	orange	see (you)	voyez
our	notre/nos	sees	voit
oyster	l'huître	sell (I)	vends
pain	la douleur	she	elle
passport	le passeport	sheep	le mouton
peach	la pêche	shoe	la chaussure
pear	la poire	shop	le magasin
pedestrian	le piéton	short	court
pen	le stylo	sister	la soeur
petrol	l'essence (f)	skirt	la jupe
piano	le piano	slow	lent
picnic	le pique-nique	small	petit
pink	rose	snail	l'escargot (m)
plate	l'assiette (f)	snow	la neige
please	s'il vous plaît	sock	la chaussette
police	la police	son	le fils
postage stamp	le timbre	soon	bientôt
potato	la pomme de terre	spanner	la clef
		speak (I)	parle
pretty	joli	spoon	la cuiller
price	le prix	staircase	l'escalier (m)
prize	le prix	station	la gare
pullover	le pullover	striker	le gréviste
quarter (of		stupid	stupide
time)	(le) quart	suitcase	la valise
quick	rapide	sun	le soleil
quiet	tranquille	table	la table
quite	assez	tablecloth	la nappe
rabbit	le lapin	telephone	le téléphone
rain	la pluie	thank you	merci
receipt	le reçu	the	le/la/les
red	rouge	theatre	le théâtre

238

there	là	wife	la femme
thief	le voleur	window	la fenêtre
thin	mince	wine	le vin
throat	la gorge	with	avec
ticket	le billet	woman	la femme
time	le temps	worker	l'ouvrier (m)
tip	le pourboire	year	l'an (m)
tired	fatigué	yellow	jaune
to	à	yes	oui
toilet	la toilette	you	vous
tomato	la tomate	young	jeune
tongue	la langue	your	votre/vos
towel	la serviette		
town	la ville		
tree	l'arbre (m)		
trousers	le pantalon	**Days of the Week**	
trout	la truite	Monday	lundi
tyre	le pneu	Tuesday	mardi
ugly	laid	Wednesday	mercredi
under	sous	Thursday	jeudi
underpants	le slip	Friday	vendredi
vegetable	le légume	Saturday	samedi
very	très	Sunday	dimanche
waiter	le garçon		
waitress	la serveuse		
walk	la promenade		
wall	le mur	**Months of the Year**	
want (I)	veux	January	janvier
want (they)	veulent	February	février
want (you)	voulez	March	mars
wants	veut	April	avril
wardrobe	l'armoire (f)	May	mai
was (he, she,		June	juin
it)	était	July	juillet
was (I)	étais	August	août
wasp	la guêpe	September	septembre
water	l'eau (f)	October	octobre
week	la semaine	November	novembre
were (they)	étaient	December	décembre
wet	mouillé		
what time	quelle heure		
is it?	est-il?		
when	quand	**Numbers**	
where	où	zero	zéro
white	blanc (blanche)	one	un
why	pourquoi	two	deux
wide	large	three	trois

four	quatre	ten	dix
five	cinq	eleven	onze
six	six	twenty	vingt
seven	sept	twenty-five	vingt-cinq
eight	huit	12 midnight	minuit
nine	neuf	12 midday	midi

LINKWORD ON COMPUTER

First Courses
*FRENCH   *GERMAN   *SPANISH   *ITALIAN
*GREEK   *RUSSIAN   *DUTCH   *PORTUGUESE

On IBM PC & COMPATIBLES, APPLE II Series and BBC Model (B) disk only.
*Also available on MACINTOSH and COMMODORE 64 (USA only).

"O" LEVEL FRENCH

An extensive vocabulary and grammar up to "O" level standard, ideal as a follow-up course to the book or first course programs or as a revision or "Brush-up" course for the rusty!

Available on IBM PC & Compatibles; Apricot and Amstrad PCW;

B.B.C. Model (B)

Follow-up courses
*FRENCH   *GERMAN   *SPANISH   *ITALIAN

These courses are ideal follow-up courses for the first book or first course computer programmes. They give a further vocabulary and basic grammar.

Available on Disk only.

All courses available from

U.K.

PERSPECTIVE SOFTWARE,
35 HEADFORT PLACE,
LONDON SW1X 7DE
TEL: 01-235 9967

LINKWORD,
41 WALTER ROAD,
SWANSEA.

U.S.A.

ARTWORX INC.,
1844 PENFIELD ROAD,
PENFIELD,
NEW YORK.
TEL: (736) 385 6120

Audio Tape

An audio tape is available as an extra learning aid to accompany this book.

It allows you to hear and to practise the correct pronunciation for all the words used on this course.

Please send a cheque or postal order for £5.95 to

Corgi/Bantam Books, Cash Sales Department,
P.O. Box 11 Falmouth, Cornwall TR10 9EW

stating which language tape(s) you require and quoting the appropriate number(s) below. All cheques and postal orders must be in £ sterling and made payable to Transworld Publishers Ltd. The above price includes postage and packaging.
Overseas Customers:
All orders add £1.50

0552 13225 X French
0552 13226 8 German
0552 13227 6 Spanish
0552 13228 4 Italian

Name (Block Letters) ....

Address ....

....

Language reference no ....

FRANCE À LA CARTE
by Richard Binns

France à la Carte is a unique guide compiled by Richard Binns and based on twenty-five years of travelling in France. Together with **French Leave 3** this book equips a tourist for the most enjoyable and exciting French holiday they have ever experienced.

The guide uses the different treasures of France under themed headings such as 'Historical Milestones Relived', 'Unknown Rivers', 'Pleasures of Nature' and 'Hidden Corners' to lead the traveller to the many different facets that France possesses.

This book is for every lover of France – the young, the not-so-young, the country-lover and sightseer, the sports enthusiast and the museum browser, the walker and the car driver. **France à la Carte** offers them all a rich feast of pleasure and discovery.

0 552 99231 3

EN ROUTE: THE FRENCH AUTOROUTE GUIDE
by Richard Binns

En Route: The French Autoroute Guide by Richard Binns is invaluable for planning a holiday or business trip in France and essential in an emergency. Over 300 French autoroute exits have been researched and mapped by the author.

The exit maps identify and locate a selection of nearby hotels and restaurants − which will suit all pockets − garages, banks, supermarkets, camping and caravanning sites, chemists, petrol stations, public telephones, post offices, car parks, tourist information offices, hospitals, churches, police stations and general shopping areas. 26 route maps show autoroute exits, adjacent main towns, toll booths, service and rest areas and facilities for the disabled.

* Easy to understand and easy to follow
* Over 10,000 pieces of information
* Feeling unwell? Locate the nearest chemist
* Car in trouble? Locate a selection of garages
* Need money fast? Locate nearest banks
* Cheaper petrol than autoroute service stations? Use off-the-autoroute stations or, better still, big supermarkets
* Hotels, restaurants with bedrooms, camping sites: all easily found without the need to buy a series of expensive large-scale maps

0 552 99234 8

A SELECTED LIST OF REFERENCE TITLES
AVAILABLE FROM CORGI BOOKS

THE PRICES SHOWN BELOW WERE CORRECT AT THE TIME OF GOING TO PRESS. HOWEVER TRANSWORLD PUBLISHERS RESERVE THE RIGHT TO SHOW NEW RETAIL PRICES ON COVERS WHICH MAY DIFFER FROM THOSE PREVIOUSLY ADVERTISED IN THE TEXT OR ELSEWHERE.

☐ 07200 1	TEST YOURSELF (I.Q.)	*William Bernard & Jules Leopold*	£1.95
☐ 09806 X	WHAT DO YOU SAY AFTER YOU SAY HELLO		
		Eric Berne M.D.	£2.95
☐ 99234 8	EN ROUTE: FRENCH AUTOROUTE GUIDE	*Richard Binns*	£3.95
☐ 99230 5	HIDDEN FRANCE	*Richard Binns*	£3.95
☐ 99231 3	FRANCE A LA CARTE	*Richard Binns*	£3.95
☐ 99232 1	FRENCH LEAVE 3	*Richard Binns*	£4.95
☐ 99233 X	RICHARD BINNS' BEST OF BRITAIN	*Richard Binns*	£3.95
☐ 12772 8	KNOW YOUR OWN PSI-Q	*Hans Eysenck & Carl Sargent*	£2.50
☐ 12555 5	IN SEARCH OF SCHRODINGER'S CAT	*John Gribbin*	£3.95
☐ 13053 2	LINKWORD LANGUAGE COURSE IN FRENCH		
		Dr. M. Gruneberg	£3.95
☐ 13054 0	LINKWORD LANGUAGE COURSE IN GERMAN		
		Dr. M. Gruneberg	£3.95
☐ 13055 9	LINKWORD LANGUAGE COURSE IN SPANISH		
		Dr. M. Gruneberg	£3.95
☐ 13056 7	LINKWORD LANGUAGE COURSE IN ITALIAN		
		Dr. M. Gruneberg	£3.95
☐ 99183 X	GUITAR	*Dan Morgan*	£4.95
☐ 12713 2	MY FAVOURITE POEM		
		Mary Wilson, Sharon Allen, Leukaemia Trust	£2.95
☐ 12623 3	THE RIGHT BRAIN EXPERIENCE	*Marilee Zdenek*	£3.95

All Corgi Books are available at your bookshop or newsagent, or can be ordered from the following address:

Corgi/Bantam Books,
Cash Sales Department,
P.O. Box 11, Falmouth, Cornwall TR10 9EN

Please send a cheque or postal order (no currency) and allow 60p for postage and packing for the first book plus 25p for the second book and 15p for each additional book ordered up to a maximum charge of £1.90 in UK.

B.F.P.O. customers please allow 60p for the first book, 25p for the second book plus 15p per copy for the next 7 books, thereafter 9p per book.

Overseas customers, including Eire, please allow £1.25 for postage and packing for the first book, 75p for the second book, and 28p for each subsequent title ordered.